A T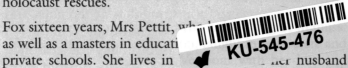

Jayne Pettit is the author of several children's books including *My Name Is San Ho*, the story of a young Vietnamese refugee and *A Place To Hide*, true stories of holocaust rescues.

Fox sixteen years, Mrs Pettit, wh̲_ _ _ as well as a masters in educati_ _ _ _ _ private schools. She lives in _ _ _ _ _ _ ᵗ̲ᵉ̲ʳ̲ ̲nusband _ _ _ p.

The photo on the front cover of this book shows children of eight years of age and older who worked as runners for ghetto organizations in Lithuania during World War II. They passed on urgent announcements and delivered warnings to members of the underground engaged in drills, to *minyans praying in secret, to food smugglers at the gate, and to others that the Germans were coming. They acted with the maturity and responsibility of seasoned members of the underground. At the bottom right is Yankele Bergman, who for three years risked his safety by carrying the photographer's diary entries, documents, and other materials from the Council offices to their hiding place.

*Minyan – means number in Hebrew. It refers to the quorum of ten men over the age of thirteen which is needed for public worship.

A Time to Fight Back

by Jayne Pettit

MACMILLAN
CHILDREN'S BOOKS

First published 1995 by Macmillan Children's Books

a division of Macmillan Publishers Limited
Cavaye Place London SW10 9PG
and Basingstoke

Associated companies throughout the world

ISBN 0 330 34133 2

1 3 5 7 9 8 6 4 2

A CIP catalogue record for this book is available from
the British Library

Phototypeset by Intype, London
Printed and bound in Great Britain by
Cox & Wyman Ltd, Reading, Berks

Acknowledgements

The author is deeply grateful to Mary Hardy, research librarian at the Howe Library in Hanover, New Hampshire for her generous assistance over the period of many months of investigation and to all of those at the Baker Library, Dartmouth College. Special thanks to Barry Van Dyck for her valuable suggestions and to Mandy Little who brought my work to the attention of Susie Gibbs and Gaby Morgan, my gracious editors at Macmillan Children's Books. And finally, a word of appreciation to my husband, Bin, for his patience, understanding and support.

To my grandchildren,
Julianne, Jeremy and Geoffrey,
Alyssa, Alexandra, and Tess.

Contents

Introduction

During the late 1920s, Adolf Hitler set the stage for a nightmare that would one day reach to the far corners of the globe. To the crowds that gathered in towns and cities throughout Germany, Hitler spoke of his dream – a Third Reich, or empire, as he called it, that would last for a thousand years.

Year by year, Hitler's influence continued to grow. By 1930, he and his followers in the National Socialist German Workers' Party (the Nazis) had won important seats in the government. By 1933, Adolf Hitler had complete control.

In the months that followed, thousands of people who opposed the Nazi regime were arrested and many were executed. Books were burned, newspapers and radio stations were nationalized, and teachers throughout the country were ordered to teach the Nazi ideology.

As Hitler and the Nazis increased their power over the people, the Jews of Germany were among the first to be persecuted, because the Nazis considered them to be an inferior race. Jewish lawyers and doctors lost their practices, and university professors were denied their positions. Forced to wear the Star of David on their clothing, Jews were no longer permitted to use public transport and their children were barred from attending school.

In 1938, Hitler and his armies marched into Austria. By the following year, Czechoslovakia and Poland had fallen to the Nazis, and in 1940, Denmark, Norway, The Netherlands and Belgium were taken over. World War II had begun in earnest. As the Nazi terror swept through country after country, Jews everywhere were cut off from the rest of society. Eventually millions of them were to die in the gas chambers.

Between 1939 and 1945, countless numbers of children suffered the hardships and the horrors of World War II. In England, more than a million children were separated from their families when they were evacuated from London and other major cities under bombardment from German air raids during the Blitz. Many of those who stayed behind were orphaned or killed.

Children in the occupied countries of Europe learned the pain of hunger and disease as the Germans confiscated food supplies, livestock and fuel to supply their own armies. Millions of children in Beligium, France, The Netherlands, Czechoslovakia and Poland were sent into slave labour in German factories. As war spread throughout Asia and the South Pacific, unaccounted numbers of children lost their lives.

In the midst of this seemingly endless night, there were children throughout Europe and elsewhere who waged their own battles against the forces of evil. In each country, young people risked their lives to carry secret messages back and forth between units working in the Resistance. Others smuggled food to people in hiding and others helped to blow up bridges and munitions factories. In Nazi-occupied Denmark, a group of brave young boys printed an underground newsletter, sabotaged enemy barracks, stole weapons and even set fire to a train carrying German military supplies!

A Time to Fight Back focuses on the experiences of six children caught in the web of World War II. In France, a deaf mute rescued an American fighter pilot whose plane had been shot down. In Belgium, a child distributed a clandestine newspaper and in Scotland, a young teenager wrote of her fears of a German invasion of her island. Of the three other children, the first spent years in hiding, the second was a prisoner at Auschwitz, and the third was a four-year-old victim of bombing raids over Germany. Each story is unique. Each is a tale of remarkable courage.

1
The Secret Courier

In May of 1940, the little country of Belgium found itself overrun by the German armies for the second time in less than twenty-five years. The people of Belgium, defiant yet powerless in the face of such an overwhelming enemy, lost no time in forming underground organizations in every village, town and city throughout the land.

During the months that followed, the Germans began mass deportations of the country's 45,000 Jews, but not without strong resistance from Belgian citizens. Men and women in every walk of life came to the rescue of thousands of Jewish men, women and children. The Dowager Queen Elizabeth of Belgium used her influence to save hundreds of Jews. Catholic and Protestant churches everywhere found hiding places for Jews in convents, monasteries and in private homes. Railway workers derailed deportation trains heading out of the country and police officers provided false identification papers for those who went into hiding. As a result of these efforts, nearly half of the total Jewish population was saved.

Soon after their arrival in Belgium, the Nazis seized control of all newspapers and radio stations in the country, cutting off vital lifelines of communication between the Belgian people and the outside world. Soon, hundreds of underground printing presses went into operation in cellars and out of the way places everywhere.

In the city of Brussels, now jammed with armed vehicles and tanks and roving units of the German secret police, twelve-year-old Peter Brouet lived with his mother and father on a quiet street not far from the historic Egmont Garden. For as long as he could remember, Peter had listened to stories of his grandfather's experiences as an editor of a secret newspaper during World War I.

There were many editors of that paper, Peter's father would tell him, because in spite of the fact that the printing presses were frequently moved in order to avoid discovery, German spies would get word of their whereabouts and destroy the equipment. The editors would then be lined up in the streets and executed. Young Peter Brouet was under no illusions about the risks involved in publishing the newspaper. His own grandfather had been one of those editors who had been shot.

The publication and distribution of *La Libre Belgique* (Free Belgium) during World War I remained a mystery to all who read it. Housewives returning from the market-place would find copies of the paper tucked into their shopping baskets. Business people and passengers on trains and trams would discover the paper smuggled into their coat pockets. Home owners leaving for work each morning would find that someone had slipped *La Libre Belgique* through their letter boxes the night before. Most amazing was the fact that even after the destruction of the paper's presses and the execution of its editors, *La Libre Belgique* would soon reappear in every corner of the city. Somehow, new equipment would go into operation, and new editors would replace those whose lives had been lost.

During World War I, *La Libre Belgique* and other papers like it became a strong link between the people of Belgium for several reasons. In addition to bringing them news from the war front or of events taking place in their country, the newspaper gave out coded information from underground resistance groups, relayed disguised messages between Belgian citizens, and urged them to band together in the cause of freedom.

The unknown editor of *La Libre Belgique* always signed himself 'Peter Pan' after the mischievous little boy in the much loved children's story, and from time to time he enjoyed playing a joke on the German oppressors. Once, he suggested to his readers that if ever they had a problem with the secret police they should contact a gentleman by the name of Monsieur Vesalius at the Place des Barricades.

As soon as he had read the article, the tyrannical commandant of the German Occupational Forces, General Friedrich von Falkenhausen, stormed to the Place des Barricades with a squad of secret police – only to find that 'Monsieur Vesalius' was nothing but a bronze statue!

Years after World War I, Peter and his father would act out the story of *La Libre* and the mysteries surrounding it. Switching roles, each would take turns at being editor, newspaper boy, or even the hated General von Falkenhausen. Each time, they would find new ways to send secret messages or hide their 'paper' in unlikely places around the house.

One day, when Peter was eight years old, he went down to his cellar and set up the toy printing press that his father and mother had given him for Christmas. He had decided to write an article about someone whose name was frequently mentioned in discussions between his parents. In the article, Peter warned the people of Belgium of a man whose armies would one day invade his country if the people weren't careful. The man was Adolf Hitler and the year was 1935.

Peter finished his work, and signing it 'Peter Pan', he put the printing press back in its secret hiding place and tiptoed up to his father's study and knocked on the door.

When Peter heard his father's voice inviting him

in, he opened the door with a great flourish and entered the room. Bowing low and clicking his heels, he addressed his father as '*Herr General*'.

Immediately recognizing the start of a new round of their old game, Monsieur Brouet spun around quickly in his chair and roared at his son: how had he, a stranger, managed to slip past the guards? And what was the reason for his presence?

Just as quickly, Peter greeted the 'General' once again, this time adding that he was the 'tailor' who had mended the 'General's' coat pocket the week before.

Continuing the game, Peter's father pretended to ignore him, but not before unbuttoning his coat pocket. With this, the boy tucked the fresh copy of *La Libre Belgique*, which he had just printed, into the gaping pocket. And as he did so, a strong arm reached out to grab him.

Accusing Peter of being an enemy spy, the 'General' pulled the paper from his jacket, read it, and threatened to deliver him to the firing squad.

When they had finished their game, Peter's father told him yet another tale of World War I and of General von Falkenhausen's troubles with *La Libre Belgique*. Each morning, as the paper found its way to the General's desk, he would go into a rage, issuing orders for the immediate arrest of the unknown editor. But despite all of the threats, General von Falkenhausen never did locate the mysterious culprit, nor did he discover who had delivered the paper. After World War I, the truth was revealed. As it happened, one of *La Libre Belgique*'s couriers was the old woman who cleaned his office. Hiding the paper in her apron, she would place it on the General's desk when she had finished her chores.

The years passed and the menace of Hitler and his followers increased. Throughout the countries of Europe, people everywhere sensed the approach of yet another war with Germany. And then, in 1938, the Nazis marched into Austria. In the following year, Czechoslovakia was taken, and then came the collapse of Poland.

On the morning of 10 May 1940, as the pale light of dawn crept across the skies, Hitler and his mighty armies invaded Belgium, Denmark, The Netherlands and tiny Luxembourg. In each country, the people put up a brave fight but they were no match for the awesome power of the German militia. World War II had begun.

Within weeks, the click of polished boots could be heard in the streets of Brussels as Nazi soldiers in smartly pressed uniforms marched through the city. Then came the roar of tanks and armoured vehicles. The people turned out by the thousands, their faces taut with hatred.

The highly organized invaders moved in quickly. Loudspeakers blasted out orders to the people, warning them of the swift arrest and immediate execution of those who tried to defy the enemy. Curfews went into effect and notices on public buildings issued rules for the rationing of food. And that was just the beginning.

By a strange twist of fate, the new commandant of

the German Occupational Forces was none other than the nephew of the dreaded General von Falkenhausen. Immediately, he ordered that any pages describing the invasion of Belgium during World War I be torn out of the school history books.

Soon after the arrival of the Germans, the Belgian people felt the grip of hunger as livestock and food supplies left the country by the trainload for delivery to the German armies and their families abroad. Each day, shopkeepers in stores everywhere struggled to find food for their customers and the queues in front of empty shop windows grew longer and longer.

The scarcity of food soon began to take a heavy toll on Belgium's school children, who often had to go to bed hungry. Many of the students, weakened from lack of nourishment, fainted in class. For Jewish children, the problem was even greater because the Germans made certain that the amount of food issued to Jewish families was substantially less than that available to other Belgians.

As matters grew worse, Peter Brouet returned from school one day and told his parents that his best friend, Jules Solomon, had fainted in class that morning. Peter was concerned and upset because Jules had refused to share Peter's lunch with him.

At dinnertime that evening, Peter's mother went next door to the Solomons' home with a small basket of food. When Madame Solomon saw the basket, she was embarrassed and vigorously protested about the offering. Finally, when Madame Brouet informed her that Jules had become ill in school that day, the

10

distraught mother gave in and accepted the basket.

Not long after this incident, Jules did not come to class one day. When school was dismissed later that afternoon, Peter ran home and hopped over the wall between his house and the Solomons' to find Jules sitting in the back yard poring over an arithmetic assignment. When Peter asked him why he hadn't been in school that day, the boy told him that General von Falkenhausen had just issued a new order. Jewish students were no longer allowed to attend school.

With that, Peter reached into his school bag and brought out his own book, some paper and two pencils. Minutes later, the two young boys were sitting together in the cellar of the Solomon home solving the problems that Peter had learned in the classroom that morning. For some days after this, Peter Brouet rushed home from school each afternoon, pulled his school books from his bag and went next door to the Solomons' cellar to teach his friend, Jules, everything that he had learned that day in class.

Then one afternoon, it happened. As neighbours up and down the quiet street watched from behind half-closed window blinds, an unmarked car pulled up to the Solomon home. The car stopped, the doors opened and from it emerged several of General von Falkenhausen's uniformed secret police. Within a short time, the Solomons – Jules, his baby sister and his parents – were seen walking down the steps of their home and ordered into the police car. The car sped off, and the Solomons were never seen again.

*

All over Belgium, people were devastated by the events that were taking place. For those who openly defied the German invaders, public executions of hundreds of Belgians took place, and many citizens began to lose hope.

And then, early one morning, men and women throughout the country awakened to find their letter boxes jammed with the pages of a newspaper. *La Libre Belgique* was back!

During the weeks and months that followed, copies of the familiar paper were distributed to homes and businesses everywhere. Just as in World War I, housewives found them in their market baskets, passengers on trains and trams discovered them in their pockets and school teachers found them on their desks. This time, however, with improved equipment and what became known as 'garages', the newspaper could be printed more efficiently. And if word reached its editors of an impending raid by the Gestapo, the presses could be quickly dismantled and whisked away by car to a new location.

Once again, Peter Brouet's father became involved with the work of *La Libre Belgique*, but in a different way. During World War I, Monsieur Brouet had been one of thousands of school children who had helped to distribute the paper. Now he was one of the editors.

One day, Monsieur Brouet came home from his shop looking worried and distressed. When his wife asked him what was troubling him, he replied that some neighbourhoods in the city were not getting

12

enough copies of the paper. Madame Brouet, who had become active in smuggling *La Libre* to women in market-places throughout Brussels, suggested that she could get additional women to help her. Monsieur Brouet agreed and added that children might also help with the work.

As time passed, the number of people involved with the distribution of the underground paper increased. But Monsieur and Madame Brouet began to notice a change in their son. Peter had grown quieter and more serious than in the past and was often away from home for hours at a time. When he did appear, he seemed tired and had little to say.

And then one morning at breakfast, Peter let his parents in on a secret. For weeks, he and a group of friends had been helping to deliver the newspaper!

Peter's parents were worried about him. They knew the risks involved in their work and the swift reprisals that followed the arrest of those who were involved in any resistance activity. It was not uncommon for children to be executed for their part in the movement. But, they reasoned, if other boys and girls were willing to take those risks, how could they prevent Peter from helping? And besides, Monsieur Brouet explained to his wife, he and his son had spent years practising for times like these. When it came to the smuggling of the newspaper, Peter had learned all of the tricks of the trade and had invented a few of his own.

The next night, as the people of Brussels lay sleeping, the sounds of air raid sirens pierced the air. Peter and his parents, awakened by the noise, hurried to their cellar. As they watched through their darkened windows, white trails of searchlights darted through the skies and the blasts of anti-aircraft guns shook the ground outside the house.

Then, from a short distance away, a lone plane dropped from the sky, its propeller sputtering and its wings in flames. Seconds later, it crashed in a brilliant burst of fire.

The next morning, the people of Brussels learned what had happened. A British airman returning from a raid over Germany had become separated from his squadron. The pilot, unable to eject from his plane, had been killed.

From all over the city men, women and children walked to the scene of the crash. In their arms they carried flowers from their gardens. Reaching the aircraft, they laid the flowers at the site, and stood with bowed heads, and hands held in tribute to their fallen ally. Each day the crowds of people increased, and each day the Germans patrolling the area grew angrier. Finally, at the orders of General von Falkenhausen, the plane was hauled away.

The following day, the lines of people who gathered at the place where the plane had been shot down increased, and fresh flowers appeared.

The young General von Falkenhausen, infuriated by the defiance of the Belgians, ordered the immediate arrest of anyone caught at the scene of the crash.

The editors of *La Libre* went into action. Throughout the city, a special edition of the newspaper appeared, telling readers to continue their act of defiance. The message to the people of Brussels was simple and direct: take to the trams.

At home, Peter and his parents worked for hours gathering bundles of copies together for distribution. Then each went their separate ways; Madame Brouet to the market-places, and Monsieur Brouet to other parts of the city. Peter waited until the evening curfew had sounded and then stole through the darkness with his group, up one street and down another, darting from doorway to doorway to push their papers through each letter box. At the sound of an approaching vehicle, the group separated, slipping into alley-ways in practised silence.

Peter and the others worked through the night to deliver the paper, running back to the house for fresh bundles when their supplies ran low. With the first light of day, they returned to their homes to catch a few brief hours of sleep.

Later that day, the Brouets left their house and walked to the nearest tram terminal where a large crowd had assembled. Quickly and quietly the people boarded one of the five trams waiting in line at the kerb. Peter and his parents moved to the fifth tram and waited for the column to progress through the city to the site of the crashed plane. Then, as each tram approached the scene, it slowed to a halt. Soon, others arrived from all over the city. Following a signal, all of the conductors switched off their engines and the people rose in silence with heads bowed and hands clasped behind them.

German soldiers swarmed around the trams, their rifle butts banging on the windows, but the people refused to budge from their positions. Furious, the soldiers demanded that the doors be opened and shouted at the conductors to move on or face arrest.

Minutes passed, and nothing happened. And then, slowly, the tram at the head of the queue began to creep forward, and then another and another until all of the trams had left the curb. The passengers continued to keep their vigil, standing silently by their seats, eyes fixed on the sentries outside.

Once again, *La Libre Belgique* had accomplished its work. Once again, the citizens of the little country of Belgium had acted together in the only way they could to defy a powerful and seemingly indestructible enemy. And Peter 'Pan' Brouet, the grandson of one of the original editors, had been a part of it all.

2
The Hidden

The people of Lublin, Poland, could trace their city's history back to medieval times when a cluster of peasants' houses and shops sprang up around the hilltop castle of the fourteenth century king, Kazimierz the Great. Several hundred years later, Lublin had developed into a thriving metropolis of 200,000 people.

One section of the city was composed of factories, stores and craft shops, along with several neighbourhoods where most of the merchants and business people lived. In addition, there was the ghetto area where a large percentage of the Jews of Lublin resided.

Although Jewish, Nechama Bawnik and her older sister lived with their parents in the prosperous and predominantly Christian area of the city. Their apartment on a side street just off the main avenue was surrounded by gracious modern buildings, tree-lined parks and shops catering to the wealthy.

Nechama's father, Roman, was a brilliant man and the owner of two factories. As a student at the university, he had once trained for the rabbinate. A highly respected member of the business community, he was known for his quiet strength and his devotion to his family.

Nechama's mother was a compassionate and deeply religious woman who clung to the traditions of the past and left the education of her daughters entirely in the hands of her husband.

Eight-year-old Nechama learned about anti-Semitism at an early age. More than once she had watched roving gangs of Polish teenagers smashing the windows of Jewish businesses and shouting obscene words at the owners inside. When Nechama discussed these happenings with her father, he would explain that many people in Poland did not think kindly of Jews. He would also tell her that being born a Jew was nothing to be ashamed of.

Nechama and her sister attended a private school in Lublin along with other students from prominent Jewish families. Unlike her sister, she was not a good student, and much preferred playing in the park while her governess met with other governesses to discuss the events of the day. Sometimes, Nechama overheard conversations about an impending war in Europe.

On Friday and Saturday evenings, Nechama's home was filled with family members and good friends who gathered regularly for discussions around a table rich with many pastries and sweets of every kind. On most occasions the talk centred around the rumours of war and Hitler's hatred of the Jews. During these discussions, Nechama stayed close to her father, who would stroke her blonde hair and kiss her gently on the top of her head.

On Friday 1 September 1939, Hitler invaded Poland and Nechama's well-protected world came to an abrupt end. Air raid sirens broke through the calm of the late summer afternoon, and just as the Bawnik family raced to the cellar of the apartment, a bomb exploded nearby, shaking the building and shattering windows.

The bombings continued for days, while the Polish army fought in vain to resist the attack. Within a week, the fighting in Lublin ended, and just as quickly, the streets of the city were swarming with German soldiers. On 17 September, Russia attacked Poland from her eastern border, and by 5 October, the country had surrendered to the Germans in the west and the Russians in the east.

An uneasy quiet followed. Nechama's father went back to his duties at the factories and the girls returned to school. But the German presence was ominous and the atmosphere was tense. Refugees from the west arrived by the hundreds with tales of German atrocities and the news circulated of Hitler's determination to rid Europe of the Jews.

Each day, the Germans tightened their hold on the Polish people, whom they considered inferior because, like other Eastern Europeans, the Polish were members of the Slavic race. The Jews, however, suffered the greatest hardships.

As Jewish businesses, stores and factories were shut down or taken over by the Germans, Nechama's parents discussed the possibility of moving the family to the Russian sector of the country where conditions at that time were less threatening. A decision was reached. Nechama's father would travel to Kovel, a Russian-occupied city, to investigate matters there.

While Mr Bawnik was away, Nechama's mother took charge of one of the family-owned factories. One morning, Mrs Bawnik reached the factory to find its doors locked and posted with German orders forbidding entrance. Knowing that one of her employees from the night shift was inside, she removed the notice, and unlocked the door in order to rescue him. With that, a Gestapo agent suddenly appeared and beat her until she fell, unconscious, to the ground. From inside the building, two factory employees watched in silence, knowing that any attempt to rescue the woman would be useless. Finally, the German left, and the men quickly opened the door, lifted their brutally battered employer into a carriage and took her home.

For a short time after the German occupation of Lublin, Nechama and her sister were tutored at home by a young woman by the name of Hela Trachtenberg who, like other Jewish teachers and university professors, had been dismissed from her position at a high school in Warsaw. The girls took to Hela instantly, and the three soon became fast friends.

Each day, for four hours, Nechama and her sister studied Latin, mathematics, science and literature. Urged on by Hela's gentle ways and soft-spoken humour, Nechama soon began to take a serious interest in her studies. But there were great risks involved. The Germans, in addition to closing the schools to Jewish students, had also banned private instruction in the home. For Nechama and anyone caught in this forbidden activity, the punishment was death by the firing squad.

Nechama's father returned from Kovel telling the family that he had decided not to move them. But months later, as the situation in Lublin worsened, he realized that his decision had been the wrong one. And with the closing of the border between the German and Russian zones, escape from Poland was now impossible.

Of the two factories owned by the Bawnik family, the larger one manufactured chemicals. With the German take-over of Jewish factories that were considered essential to the war effort, a German commissioner was appointed to supervise operations at the chemical factory. Nechama's father refused to work for him and left the company.

As time went by, however, it became obvious that work was a matter of life and death. Those Jews who had been unable to find new employment were often sent off to German labour camps. Others simply disappeared. Nechama's father soon came to realize that for the safety of his family, he would have to get work at the chemical factory.

When Mr Bawnik went to see the German commissioner, he was told that he had come too late and that all of the jobs were filled. A long silence followed, and finally, without further comment, Mr Bawnik got up from his chair to leave. But as he reached the office door, the German suddenly changed his mind. A job could be found after all, and the identification papers so necessary for survival would be provided.

With her husband now employed at the factory, Mrs Bawnik decided that for further protection of her family, she too would look for work. Finding a job as a housekeeper for a high ranking Nazi officer, she proved herself to be such a fine worker that her employers took to giving her food baskets to supplement the meagre provisions available in the stores.

Conditions in the city of Lublin were becoming desperate. From conversations that she overheard in her employers' house, Nechama's mother learned of increased deportations, executions and disappearances. Jewish homes were frequently raided and robbed of jewellery, china and silver. Finally, the section of the city in which Nechama and her family lived became forbidden to Jews under an edict called *Judenrein*, or 'cleansing the country of Jews'. Having nowhere to go, the Bawniks were offered a room that was one of three in an apartment in the Jewish quarter of the city. In time, more people arrived to settle into the other two rooms. A tiny kitchen was shared by the three families.

One evening, Nechama's mother rushed back to the Jewish quarter with alarming news. That day at work, the German officer's wife had told her that she could no longer employ her. Then, in a sobbing voice, the woman had warned her of a raid that would take place later that night.

After a few brief words, Nechama's parents gathered together what few items they could carry, including the heavy coats into which Nechama's mother had sewn money and all of the family jewellery. Minutes later, Nechama, her sister and her parents left the little room that had been their brief home and walked silently into the darkness.

Later, at the chemical factory, the German commissioner greeted Nechama and her family kindly and promised that he would protect them. A large, empty room on the second floor would provide a safe hiding place and in the morning Nechama's mother and sister would be given work in the factory. All would be well, he assured everyone.

As the commissioner turned to leave, Mr Bawnik pulled from his coat pocket a small cloth bag containing jewellery and gold. Presenting it to the German, Nechama's father asked that it be kept for future use in case of trouble. The official agreed that he would return the bag if it were needed.

A Polish caretaker who lived in the building with

his wife brought mattresses for the family to sleep on until he could find a few additional furnishings for them. Everyone settled themselves gratefully and tried not to think of what might be happening back in the ghetto.

The next morning, Nechama and the others learned what had happened. Soon after they had escaped to the factory, German SS troops had stormed into the ghetto and ordered the entire Jewish population into the streets. There, the sick and the lame had been shot first. Then, as in all raids, families had been separated from one another and babies taken from their mothers. Beatings had followed and those who could no longer stand had also been shot. Of those who remained, the wounded had been deported to concentration camps, and the rest had been sent to a new labour camp called Majdan Tatarski. Hela Trachtenberg, Nechama's beloved friend and tutor, had been transported to the labour camp.

For the next year, Nechama and her family continued to live in the deserted room at the factory. Her parents and her sister worked long hours and the days were empty and lonely. Outside, Nechama could hear the sounds of children's voices as they played in a school yard not far from the building. For a time, the sounds of the pupils' laughter provided comfort and served as a reminder of the happy life she had once led. But soon, the voices began to depress her and made her fearful of what the future might bring.

*

The year 1942 was drawing to a close. During the time that Nechama and her family sheltered at the factory, one disaster followed another. Many of Nechama's relatives throughout Poland had either lost their lives or had been deported. And during a raid on the labour camp at Majdan Tatarski, Hela Trachtenberg had been beaten and shot to death.

As these events unfolded, Nechama's father came to the conclusion that the only way the family could survive would be to go into hiding in Warsaw. There, with the help of a Polish Christian, they might be able to live out the war.

Then one day, a cousin who lived in Warsaw visited the factory and offered the Bawniks space in his apartment there. The cousin, although Jewish, had amassed a small fortune in undercover business dealings with a number of German officers. Because of his connections, the cousin told Nechama's father that he could provide them with a safe hiding place.

After two days of discussions, the plans to go into hiding in Warsaw were finalized. A short time later, carrying false papers and new names which identified them as Christian Poles, Nechama and her family were on their way.

Nechama's cousin, Bolek, was a big, cheerful man with a ready smile and exuberant ways, and lived in an expensively furnished apartment on one of Warsaw's finest streets. Nechama and her family were given a room in which to live and a kitchen that they were to share with several other people who had moved in.

After several days of watching families come and go, Nechama and her family learned that Bolek's apartment had become a processing centre for Jews searching for a safe place to live. Bolek supplied food and false identification papers to all who needed them and a bed on which to sleep until living arrangements could be made.

During the next few days, the rules for survival had to be learned. Names, birth dates and birth places were practised, and under no circumstances could actual names be used. Family background, relatives and occupations were fictionalized for extra protection in the event of interrogation.

Because they were 'passing' as Christian Poles, Nechama and her family had to memorize the prayers, doctrines and rituals of the Catholic church. This took time but was an essential part of the conversion process. It was well known that many Jews had lost their lives because they had failed to learn these facts. Everyone practised in earnest and tested one another repeatedly. The slightest mistake or hesitation could mean death or deportation.

In time, Nechama's father, ever cautious and on the alert, grew anxious about the living situation in Bolek's apartment. With so many people moving in and out, one slip-up could mean disaster. If someone in the apartment were arrested, the names of all of the others staying there might be revealed. Nechama's father was also concerned about Bolek's dealings with the Germans, and with the fact that Warsaw had become a centre for Jews going into hiding.

Bolek, as understanding as always, set out to find a house outside the city. After considerable searching, he found a couple who would take the risk of hiding the Jewish family for an exorbitant sum. Nechama's parents agreed to pay the price of protection.

The couple, Jan and Magda, lived in a tiny, two room apartment just outside Warsaw. There were two advantages to the situation: the couple had no children and no one ever visited.

The Bawniks moved into one of the two rooms and tried to settle themselves. Nechama's father was the only member of the family to venture out of the apartment. His blond hair and light blue eyes belied his Jewish heritage. Through contacts he had made with people in Warsaw, he was able to keep in touch with events as they were occurring.

Returning to the apartment one evening, Mr Bawnik told of the death of his friend and former partner back in Lublin. His daughter and son-in-law had also been in hiding in Warsaw. Later on, they were also killed.

The strain of living with Jan and Magda slowly began to affect everyone. Jan, an unemployed labourer with a violent temper, constantly fought with his wife. There were frequent beatings, and Magda's face was ringed with bruises.

On his travels out of the apartment, Nechama's father once again began the search for another place for the family to hide. Eventually, he learned from a friend that a couple in the little village of Otwock would take Nechama and her sister – again for a huge sum of money. Plans were made for the girls to travel by train, with their father coming each weekend to visit them.

At the news that the family was going to be separated the girls were extremely upset, and Nechama especially so. But left with no alternative, they knew that they must agree to their parents' wishes.

Arriving in Otwock, Nechama and her sister were relieved by the peaceful isolation of the little village. Surrounded as it was by dense forestation, Otwock seemed to offer them the protection that they needed. Following the directions that their parents had given them, the girls walked through the village until they came to the address.

A woman named Marta opened the door, and in a cold and distant manner, pointed to two very shy children, introducing them as Jurek and Ania. Nechama looked at the squalor that surrounded her. Marta's home consisted of a kitchen and one large room. In one corner stood a stove and a clothes cabinet. Beds rested in the other three corners. From the ceiling a bare light bulb cut through the otherwise dark and dingy living quarters. The only other furniture consisted of an old table and chairs.

Marta's husband, Tosiek, was a kind and generous man. Because of his work, he was away from the house from early in the morning until late in the evening. At the sound of his voice, his otherwise sullen children ran to the door and jumped into his arms. Much laughter and play followed until the family sat down to a meagre supper of soup. With Tosiek's arrival, the atmosphere brightened and the tension created by Marta's brooding manner diminished.

Because of the family's impoverished circumstances, there was little to eat and Nechama and her sister were constantly hungry. Breakfast consisted of a cup of coffee and a piece of dark bread. After that there was nothing to eat until evening when a bowl of soup was served.

To fill the empty days, Nechama and her sister took long walks through the village and the surrounding forest. It helped to get away from Marta and her gloominess and to share quiet hours and secret thoughts. Occasionally the girls allowed themselves a trip to the bakery for rolls. On these trips, Nechama and her sister tried not to think of the pain of being separated from their parents. Both fought off the possibility that they might never see them again.

When Nechama's father came to visit, he would speak of the increasingly desperate situation in Warsaw. He and his wife had been forced to move from one hiding place to another. Hearing this news, Nechama worried about her parents' safety.

In time, Nechama's father learned of some people in the city of Kielce who, in exchange for money, would find room in their home for the Bawniks. Plans were made for Nechama's sister to go to Kielce with a young man named Wojtek, to meet the family.

Then Wojtek would go to Warsaw to accompany Nechama's parents to Kielce. Nechama was to stay with Marta and her husband until it was safe enough for her to travel to Kielce.

On the day that Nechama's father visited her for the last time in Otwock, he carefully went over the steps that were to be taken. Cautioning her that she must not tell anyone of the family's plans or of where they were going, he reminded her of the gold and jewellery that was sewn into her coat. Only in the event of an emergency was Nechama to use it. For a brief moment the next morning, Nechama and her father held on to each other. Then he was gone.

Nechama stood at the window and watched him hurry down the street. Tears spilled down her cheeks and her whole body ached with the knowledge that she was alone. She had tried hard not to let her father see her fear and had not allowed herself to cry in his presence.

Nechama missed her sister. Together, they had always been able to give each other support. Now, all of that had changed.

As the days dragged by, Nechama began to wonder if she would ever be reunited with her family. She felt lost and fearful of the future, and longed for the warmth and security of the life she had once lived.

Tosiek sensed Nechama's anxieties and did whatever he could to ease her pain by reassuring her that everything would be all right. Soon, Nechama began to rely on Tosiek's friendship. In the evenings, she would wait for his return and for his fun-loving chatter at the supper table.

One day, after Marta had left the house, Nechama lost her battle with her constant hunger, and carved off a thin sliver of bread from a loaf resting on the table. When Marta returned, she immediately discovered the missing piece and went into a rage. Sometime later, Nechama learned how the woman had recognized that the bread was missing: along the edge of the loaf, Marta had carved a series of crosses so that if Nechama were to cut off a slice, the crosses would be cut off, too.

After the incident with the bread, Marta's treatment of Nechama took a turn for the worse. Nothing that the child did could please her, and the slightest mistake in the way Nechama did her chores caused the woman to explode with anger.

In her loneliness, Nechama began having nightmares about her family. Every night she would dream that her parents and her sister had disappeared and that she would never see them again. And then one wonderful night, Nechama's sister returned for her at last.

The apartment in Kielce consisted of two rooms, which housed Nechama, her family and eight other people. There was electricity but no running water and no toilet. To get water, Nechama and the others drew water from a well. An outhouse at the back of the building served as the toilet facility.

In their new hiding place, the presence of

Nechama's parents was to be kept secret. The two girls were to act as orphans related to the people with whom they were staying. Nechama and her sister would be the only members of their family to leave the house. In the event of a raid, Nechama's parents would go into a special hiding place in the apartment.

Unable to leave the apartment, Nechama's parents tried to find things to do. Nechama's mother kept busy with her cooking, and her father passed the time reading Russian or Polish classics that she brought from the library. Reunited with her family, Nechama grew stronger and was soon reading books of her own.

As time passed, the few clothes that the Bawnik family had brought with them became worn and covered with patches. Each owned one pair of shoes, and these had to be resoled many times. But they were together, and that was all that mattered.

The people in Wojtek's family were kind as well as friendly, although, like most Polish Christians, they were fiercely anti-Semitic. Nechama was disturbed by their attitude and confused by the fact that despite their feelings, they were nevertheless willing to hide Jews in their home.

In exchange for this protection, Nechama's father had to pay for food for everyone in the apartment and was also responsible for the rent. To get the money, jewellery would be exchanged on the black market. To make the money last, Nechama's father was careful to use the money only to fulfil his obligations to Wojtek and his family.

*

After Nechama and her family had been living in Kielce for some time, the Nazis in the city began stepping up their raids. At the beginning, the raids took place in public areas, but soon the Germans began searching homes as well. It was decided that in the event of such a raid, Nechama's parents would hide in the storage cellar beneath the floor of the apartment.

Late in 1943, when it became clear that the war was not going well for the Germans, the Polish underground movement surged with activity, blowing up bridges and trains in and around the city. In return for the sabotage, the Nazis increased the number of their raids and deportations of Jews.

Because of the increased risks of discovery, Nechama and her family, together with some of Wojtek's family, moved to an apartment in the neighbourhood that was more secluded, and at once set about building a shelter beneath the floorboards. An old trunk was placed over the shelter to hide the marks where the boards had been cut.

Soon after the family had moved to the new apartment, one of Wojtek's relatives came to warn them of a raid by the Nazis. Immediately, Nechama's parents rushed to the hiding place and slipped through the tiny opening one at a time. No sooner had Nechama covered the shelter with the trunk, than the Nazis rushed into the apartment and began going through closets and checking under beds. As the search continued, one of the Nazis walked over to the area where the trunk lay. Suddenly, Nechama's father coughed. The Nazi stopped and turned in the direction of the cough. Nechama stared at the wall, trying to keep her face free of expression. When no further sound was heard, the soldier gave the girl a strange little smile, and without mentioning the incident, left with the others.

As time passed, the Bawniks' funds began to run dangerously low and Nechama's father asked Wojtek if he would go back to Lublin to recover the little bag that had been given to the German commissioner at the factory for safe keeping. Wojtek agreed to make the trip, and returned soon after with the money, but with the tragic news of Bolek's death.

In January of 1945, the Germans in Poland were pushed back further and further by the advancing Russian army. With each passing day, the Bawnik family's hopes of survival increased.

And then one night, the bombings began. Nechama and her sister, along with their parents, who had not left their hiding place for what seemed like an eternity, raced to an air raid shelter. There, huddled together, they waited out the night.

At daybreak the next morning, the bombings stopped and all was quiet. Returning to the apartment, Nechama and her family caught sight of the first Russian soldiers moving down the street. The long ordeal was over.

3
City in Flames

Before the bombs fell, Königsberg was a lovely old city, Karla's mother once said. The grace of the river Pregel as it meandered past beautiful old buildings steeped in history; the swans on the castle pond; the promenade and the confectioners' shops with their little café tables crowded with people. Königsberg . . .

In the afternoons there were excursions through the city on the trams, and puppet theatres and concerts for the children. In the evenings, there were more concerts for the adults and much entertaining among friends. A cultural life like this could help one forget what was happening to one's country and its people.

Karla's home, located on the river Pregel, was filled with women. Her father, Hugo, a kind and cheerful man, was away at war. Older than her mother by

35

twenty years, Hugo Poewe had been a successful businessman before being summoned for compulsory military service.

In addition to Karla and her mother, there was Gudi, her younger sister, their nanny, Aunt Trudi, Bertha the cook and Hedwig the housekeeper.

Karla's mother was a small, beautiful young woman. An affectionate and caring mother, she spent a lot of time with her children, taking them on walks and weaving the most wonderful fairy tales as they wandered along the river front.

And then, suddenly, in the winter of 1945, Königsberg was in flames. As bombs rained down from the sky buildings turned to rubble, and the women and children of the city took to the streets. Karla and Gudi found themselves swept up by their mother and Aunt Trudi, and together the four raced to the castle pond. Near the water's edge they stood, hand in hand, choking on the suffocating air, ready to jump if they had to. Better to drown than to burn to death.

Karla's grandmother, Omi, was a woman of great wisdom and faith. She was a devout Catholic and she was fiercely independent. Raised on a farm near the Russian border in East Prussia, she had no time for Adolf Hitler, 'that lackey from Austria' who had answers for all of Germany's ills following its bitter defeat in World War I. Hitler and his rabble had toppled the genteel, but weary Hindenburg, creating a world that would one day lie in ruin. That was a certainty. Omi knew about such things.

For weeks, the bombings continued. Around her in a crowded basement shelter, Karla listened to the sobbing of the old people. And as she huddled next to her mother and the others, she heard her own voice rise with the screams of the children. There was no food, no water, no sleep. Only the deafening noise, the blinding light and the ceaseless roar of planes over Königsberg.

Sometimes, during a lull, Karla's mother or Aunt Trudi would go into the streets to find something to eat. Eventually, they learned to survive on sorrel, tree bark or a rare crust of a black bun. Karla's mother had a friend who was a pharmacist. From her, she obtained some cod liver oil. That, her mother said, helped to keep them alive.

The train moved through the countryside, bound for Dresden. Karla, Gudi, her mother and Aunt Trudi were among the passengers jammed into every available seat and space, travelling for hours through the darkness. At last, the train stopped and everyone followed the orders to get out. As the cold whipped through their clothing, the women and children ran for the protection of the bushes. Then, back on the train, back to the hunger and the fear.

The passengers on the train lost all sense of time and place. As the bombings continued, they found themselves moving forwards and then backwards, shunted from one train track to another, stopping and then starting again, lumbering on through the desolation that lay about them.

At last, the train was nearing Dresden, the one great German city that had remained untouched by Allied attack. A centre of history and art and treasures of the past, it was believed by many to be the safest of places – some called it a national air raid shelter.

On the night of 13 February 1945, less than three months before the end of the war, Dresden was hit. As the train carrying Karla and the others moved through the darkness towards the city, rumblings were heard in the distance. Explosions and fires followed. The train came to a halt, moved ahead, then stopped again. Once more, they were changed to another track. Once more, the endless journey in the opposite direction.

Thousands of people died in Dresden that night. And in the days to come, thousands more would be lost as firestorms consumed the city.

The train moved southward to Netzschkau, near the city of Plauen. Karla Poewe and her family found shelter in another crowded basement. Wrapped in her blanket, the little girl listened as her mother tried to comfort her with a fairy tale. Outside, a convoy of trucks could be heard passing through the street. Karla's mother stood and parted a covering over the window just wide enough to see tall, dark soldiers riding on their carriers. The Americans were arriving.

Years later, Karla Poewe remembered that basement in Netzschkau – the darkness, the stench and the moans of the dying. As bodies were removed, others replaced them on the floor. Each day, Karla's mother and Aunt Trudi would go into the streets to forage for food, leaving the two children in the care of a cousin. Karla, four and a half years old at the time, had stopped speaking.

After weeks in Netzschkau, Karla's mother received a letter from her husband and learned that he had been taken prisoner by the Russians. On the slightest chance that his release might eventually bring him to Netzschkau, she knew that she had to wait for him. But conditions at the shelter had become intolerable and disease was spreading. Desperate for the safety of her children, Karla's mother made the painful decision to place her children in an orphanage near Berlin. Despite the weeks and perhaps months that they would be separated from one another, the orphanage offered the only hope for her children's survival. There was no other choice.

After months in the orphanage, Karla and Gudi were reunited with their mother. But Karla had grown thin and frail. Food held no interest for her and she continued to find it difficult to speak. Karla was sent to stay with her grandmother, who had found shelter in the British sector near Hamburg. The war was over, a few potatoes were available along with a little bread, and refugees could find a room here and there.

With Omi's loving care, Karla grew stronger each day, although she missed her mother and Gudi and Aunt Trudi. When she had difficulty swallowing her food, Omi would play singing games with her.

Each Sunday, and sometimes during the week, Karla walked to the Catholic church with Omi. Afterwards, they would visit the gypsies and Omi would have her fortune read. A strong believer in both Jesus and the cards, the old woman would ask the gypsies about her six handsome sons who had gone off to the war.

Karla's grandmother was a great storyteller like her mother. But instead of fairy tales, Omi created her own stories that took Karla to mythical worlds beyond worlds. A walk in the woods could turn into a magic carpet ride. With these stories, the little girl's fears diminished, if only for moments at a time.

As summer drew to a close, Omi and Karla worked on the local farms to gather the harvest. In return, they would be given vegetables that could not be sold in the market-place. Corn husks would be dried and pounded into a crude flour, from which Omi would make thick soups and little pancakes.

With Omi, Karla learned to forage in the meadows, gathering dandelion and lime tree leaves. Berries would be found in season, and wild plums and hazel-nuts. When acorns fell from the giant oaks, they would take them to the pig farmers and receive food in exchange. Life with Omi gave balance to Karla's world. They worked hard, and received something for that work. And in between the work, there were Omi's songs and stories and fragments of peace amidst the rubble of the war's remains.

After several months with Omi, Karla grew stronger

and went back to live with her mother and the others who had moved into two rooms on the second floor of a house in the village of Werdau. While Karla's mother went foraging for food, the little girl would walk by the river with a doll that her mother had made out of remnants of material she had found.

One day as Karla was walking, a child approached her and stared longingly at the doll.

'If you let me play with your doll, I'll give you a doll's pram,' she said one morning.

Karla nodded her head, handing her doll to the other little girl.

Each day for some time, the girls would meet and Karla would hand her doll to the other child, expecting to see the pram that had been promised. But the pram never appeared.

Finally, as the child was leaving one day, Karla tried to follow her, but the child outran her. Returning home, she asked a neighbour if she knew where the stranger lived and found out that she lived in a building up on the hill.

Karla found the little girl living in one of several bombed-out buildings. Few windows remained and doors opened on to filth and emptiness. The little girl emerged from one of the buildings and came towards Karla. Her dress was ragged and torn, and her face was sad. As they talked, Karla discovered the truth about the child. Her father had been killed and her sister and brother were dead. Her mother was in an asylum. And there was no doll's pram.

As the months went by, Karla grew sickly again, and

an aunt was summoned to take her back to Omi.

On a warm summer day, Karla and her aunt set out on their journey. After several changes, they found a bus that took them close to the border of the British sector outside Hamburg. Slowly and carefully they walked to the barrier where a Russian soldier stood guard.

The barrier was lowered and Karla's aunt was asked to hand over their identification papers. Examining them, the guard told the two that they would have to wait.

In a nearby wooded area, Karla and her aunt spotted a large crowd of people being herded together by a number of Russian soldiers. Shots were fired. Those who remained standing were taken away.

The guard at the barrier was called away, and quickly handed the papers back to Karla's aunt, again ordering her to wait. After a few minutes, a voice called to them. Looking around, Karla and her aunt saw a German soldier sitting alone on a rock.

'What are you waiting for?' the soldier whispered. 'You have your papers. For heaven's sake, move on!'

Karla's aunt hesitated, not knowing what to do.

'If you walk fast, you can catch the French bus,' the man continued. 'Do you want to go to Siberia?'

Rushing towards the bus, Karla's aunt pulled her along until they saw the bus approaching. When it didn't appear to be slowing down, the woman ran to the middle of the road to force the bus to stop. The door burst open and the driver shouted that the bus was full. But Karla's aunt stood her ground, protesting that if he didn't take the child and her, they would be killed by the Russians. With this, the bus driver gave in and allowed Karla and her aunt to get on. As the vehicle moved slowly down the road, they heard a shot. Looking back, they saw the German soldier lying on the road beside the Russian check-point.

One day, Omi took Karla to see her aunt, who had found a place to live nearby. There was someone she was about to meet, Omi said cheerfully as the two walked along the street.

Arriving at her aunt's, Karla found herself standing in front of a tall, frail-looking man with dark circles under his eyes. The man was Karla's father.

On 20 May 1948, after nine months in hospital, Karla's father died. Her mother had waited for his return since 1943 when, like many other older men, he had been called up to replace the thousands of soldiers whose deaths had inflicted heavy tolls on the German army. Imprisoned by the Russians towards the end of the war, he had become gravely ill, and when it was certain that he would not recover, he had been released.

During the months that followed the death of Karla's father, her mother tried repeatedly to get identification papers that would allow her to take her children north to the British sector in Buxtehude, not far from Hamburg. Day after day, she went to the Russian authorities to ask for the papers, and each time she was refused.

To support her family, the woman who had once loved the theatre and the arts and beautiful parties, took a job selling ice-cream at a nearby entertainment park. And then one day, after months of delay, the identification papers came through.

Overjoyed, Karla's mother lost no time in packing the few clothes the family now owned and the three set out on their journey northwards. Since few buses or trams were running, and trains carrying refugees were overloaded, Mrs Poewe and her two little girls walked most of the way. Karla and Gudi each had their little bundles to carry, and their mother had an old piece of luggage she had found.

In order to avoid the crowds, the three usually travelled at night, stopping occasionally to rest and hunt for food. Karla's feet hurt as she and Gudi walked along but she didn't complain: the three of them were safe and they were together. And as she looked into her mother's eyes she could see that they were bright and full of hope.

Finally, on 1 October, Karla and her mother and sister arrived at the check-point of the British sector. Their papers were stamped and they were each given tea. It was warm and sweet.

At first, Karla and her mother and Gudi lived in a single room in Buxtehude, with Omi and another aunt. The two girls slept in a closet and the three women used the bed. But after a time, Omi moved out and Karla's mother found work which enabled her to rent three rooms in the city. One big room held a large stove and was used as a kitchen, dining room and living room. The other two rooms served as bedrooms. For the first time since they could remember, Karla and her sister had a room of their own.

One day, Karla and Gudi prepared for their first day of school. They were excited but frightened. Because of the war and their years of travelling from place to place they had never been able to attend classes.

After school that afternoon, Karla stood waiting for Gudi to come out of the building. A group of students gathered around her and began teasing her because she was so big for her class. Then the children began pointing their fingers at her, calling her a '*Flüchtling, Flüchtling*!' A refugee, a refugee . . .

In Herr Broden's class, Karla struggled to shape her letters just the right way. And when called upon, she could only whisper her answers. When she remained silent, she received a rap on the knuckles with the stick.

During arithmetic class, Herr Broden would assign a set of problems to the students and then sit back to play the violin which was always on his desk. A severe and withdrawn man with a faraway look in his eyes, Herr Broden was at once frightening and puzzling. But when he played his violin his whole countenance changed and his melodies were soft and beautiful.

One morning in class, Herr Broden discovered that his stick had been broken and asked who had

45

done it. No one answered. Again, the teacher challenged the students. Finally, when Karla became upset with the repeated questioning, Herr Broden came to the conclusion that it had been she who had broken the stick. Summoned to the front of the room, Karla was told to bend over, and when she did so, she was struck repeatedly with the broken stick.

Throughout the morning Karla had to remain standing with her face to the wall. The class giggled and she was angry and humiliated. In her fright, she had once more lost her voice and could say nothing to defend herself.

Later that day, a boy in the class stood up and admitted to Herr Broden that he had broken the stick. With that, the teacher ordered the boy to another corner. Karla was not released from her position at the wall until school was dismissed.

That evening at home, Karla told her mother what had happened in school. The next morning, she was too ill to go to class.

Sometime after that, Karla's mother accompanied her to the school and had a conference with the principal and Herr Broden. As Karla stood aside, her mother explained all that had happened to her children during the war and asked Herr Broden to be more understanding of her daughter.

In the weeks that followed, Karla found out why Herr Broden behaved the way he did. Years before, during the bombing of Dresden, Herr Broden had witnessed the death of his wife and daughter. As bombs continued to fall on the city, the two had panicked and run out into the streets. Herr Broden ran after them, only to watch them consumed by the flames of the firestorm.

In the principal's office one morning, Karla was introduced to a kind-looking man with bright, friendly eyes and a warm smile. His name was Herr Deckwerth and he was to be her new teacher.

'There is someone I want you to meet,' Herr Deckwerth told Karla. 'It's my son. You and he must spend some time together.'

After school, Karla walked with Herr Deckwerth to his home. There, she met his wife, a beautiful woman with long dark hair braided into a double ring about her head. The atmosphere in the home was happy and loving.

Karla was introduced to Benjamin, the couple's son. Coming into the room slowly on thin, weak legs encased in heavy braces, the boy struggled to put one foot in front of the other. As he approached his father eagerly, he spoke a garble of unintelligible words. But the light in his eyes was full of love.

When the boy reached his father, Karla was told that he was nine, the same age as she. A victim of polio, he was badly deformed, Herr Deckwerth said, but despite his handicaps he wanted to learn how to do things himself.

Karla's new teacher asked his son if he wanted to try to walk towards her. Benjamin turned and laboured towards her and at last reached the place where she was standing. Just as he was about to fall, Karla caught him. The boy laughed and spoke several incoherent words to her, and Karla suddenly found herself speaking out loud for the first time in years. Herr Deckwerth hugged his wife and Karla couldn't believe how happy and safe she felt.

Karla visited Benjamin Deckwerth three times a week. With each visit, she would help him to practise his walking. Then, she would put objects in the boy's hands and tell him how to say the names of the objects. Gradually, the boy's legs grew stronger and he was able to speak more clearly. And all the time, Karla kept talking, hearing the sounds of her own voice as she spoke to her new and very special friend.

In class with Herr Deckwerth, Karla learned to paint pictures. Soon, she began to create scenes that were remarkable in their beauty. Herr Deckwerth praised her work, and in time, the paintings began to draw the attention of her classmates and other teachers in the building.

One day, Karla drew a picture that pleased her teacher so much that he decided to enter it in a contest sponsored by UNICEF, the United Nations childrens' organization. Karla's painting won first prize in the contest and it was later exhibited in more than forty countries around the world.

In class, the little girl learned to write poems and to recite them aloud. These, too, showed promise and were entered into school contests. On the day of the dedication of the rebuilding of her school,

Karla was chosen to recite the poem that she had written for the ceremony.

As she was called to the podium, she stood before the microphone and looked out on to an audience crowded with parents and schoolchildren. Her legs felt weak and a shudder went through her. Would she be able to speak?

The people waited in silence for her to begin. Seconds passed. And then, as if from the distance, Karla heard her voice, high and unnatural at first but gradually gaining in strength and fluidity.

'The nightingale is very ugly,' Omi would always say. 'But when it sings it melts our hearts.' That day, Karla Poewe was the nightingale. The only difference was that, unlike the lonely songster of the night, she had grown quite beautiful indeed.

4
Sea Watch

Several miles north of Scotland, a group of islands known as the Orkneys stretch out like stepping stones across the waters of the Atlantic. Thousands of years ago, ancient tribes built mysterious stone megaliths, underground burial chambers and houses complete with adjoining passageways, stone beds and fire-places. In the ninth century, men from Norway and Denmark arrived, settling in the Orkneys and their neighbouring islands, the Shetlands, for five hundred years.

Ringed by rugged cliffs, quiet coves and harbours, the Orkneys are home to hundreds of species of birds. In the springtime, seals bask on low-lying rocks at the edge of the sea. Despite their northerly location, the climate on the Orkneys is relatively mild, due to the influence of Gulf Stream currents.

During the months between 1939 and 1940, the period known as the Phoney War, German planes swept across the skies above the Orkneys, and submarines moved soundlessly through the surrounding waters. To most of the islanders it seemed clear that Hitler was planning to invade the British Isles.

By the late summer of 1939, events were moving quickly. After Hitler's invasion of Poland on 1 September, Prime Minister Neville Chamberlain appointed Winston Churchill to the Cabinet as First Lord of the Admiralty. Two days later, after the sinking of the British passenger ship *Athenia*, Parliament declared war on Germany.

From September 1939 to May 1940, sixteen-year-old Bessie Shea kept a diary of the events as they occurred, and of her experiences and feelings about the progress of the war. From her farm home on Mainland, the largest island in the Orkneys, Bessie wrote of air raids over the capital town of nearby Kirkwall and of attacks on the Naval Base at Scapa Flow.

Bessie's story began with the sighting of the first German submarine on 5 September 1940. On that same day, three enemy spies were caught on her island.

On the following day, as the young girl was taking the cattle out of the byre, she heard the sound of aircraft. Looking up, she spotted nineteen anti-aircraft shells exploding over Kirkwall.

In her next entry, Bessie noted the capture of two

German ships. One ship was sunk and the crews of both vessels were taken prisoner. Three seamen managed to escape, however, slipping away in a motor boat. Two of the islanders gave chase, discovering the Germans the next morning in the harbour of a neighbouring island. Pulling up alongside the Germans, the islanders found them to be friendly and offered them cigarettes and a pot of tea while waiting for an armed British patroller to pick them up. But before the young Germans got their tea, the patroller arrived and took them aboard at gunpoint!

In October, Britain had initiated bombing raids on German naval bases, sunk its first enemy submarine and sent its Expeditionary Forces into Dunkirk, France. Hitler, in the meantime, was threatening to bomb every civilian town in Britain and to sink every ship in the Royal Navy. In her diary, Bessie recorded the visits to Kirkwall and to Scapa Flow by King George and Winston Churchill, who had ordered that additional anti-aircraft artillery be posted along Mainland's shores.

Summer, with its rumours of an impending invasion and its accompanying anxieties, had come to an end. And so Bessie realized that the activities she had so enjoyed – the dances and Bible class trips – would be a thing of the past for a long time. Britain was at war.

On 14 October, the Germans conducted a massive air raid on the Naval Base at Scapa Flow, sinking the *Royal Oak*, the country's most powerful warship. In the attack, eight hundred young seamen in training went down with their ship.

During the following month, the Germans began bombing the Shetlands, and a spy who had reportedly been poisoning the water supply was captured on the island of Flotta. Later, Bessie noted that three German seamen, adrift without food or water for several days, had been captured near Fife.

By mid-November, air raids throughout the Orkneys had become a common occurrence and naval battles in the North Atlantic had begun. Bessie and her family had learned to recognize the sounds of German planes as they flew over Kirkwall and Scapa Flow, a clacking noise very different from the drone of Britain's aircraft.

As the days progressed, however, the routines of everyday life had changed little. The cattle still had to be milked and farm chores completed. In the local shops, food was still plentiful.

On 22 November, as the clack-clacking of an enemy aircraft approached, Bessie grabbed the family binoculars and ran outside. As she fixed her sights, she saw a broad-winged monoplane with a black cross on the side. The plane flew overhead, passed southward, then turned and circled above her head. Minutes later, the plane was over Kirkwall and anti-aircraft guns blasted away while a British destroyer took up the chase.

During the last week of November, as the battle in the North Atlantic increased, debris from sunken ships drifted on to the beaches at Scapa Flow. One morning, Bessie wrote that she had found 'a good box'. Later that afternoon, she returned to the beach to find a wooden plank and what she called 'some oddments'.

In her walks along the beach, Bessie frequently spotted the periscopes of German submarines rising above the water. She had also learned that listening posts for enemy aircraft had been set into place throughout the Orkneys.

On 3 December, Bessie recounted an adventure which gave her cause to believe that 'not all Germans [were] bad'. In her diary, she noted that an enemy submarine had just torpedoed a British ship, forcing her crew to take to their lifeboats. As the vessel sank into the sea, the submarine surfaced, opened its hatch and offered hot food and drinks to the crewmen, who by now were soaked and shivering in the bitter Atlantic winds. Then, keeping a close watch on the men, the Germans waited until a British destroyer came to the rescue. As the submarine moved off, the ship's commander called out, 'Tell Churchill that there's still *some* humanity!'

On 17 December, Canadian troops started to arrive in Britain and air training went into full force. One week later, the first squadron of Australian airmen received their assignments.

By January, the war effort was well underway, and government rationing of butter, meat, bacon and sugar went into effect. Belgium and The Netherlands prepared for the inevitable German invasion. At the same time, Bessie and many other Orcadians were convinced that they, too, were about to be invaded.

On 22 January, an entry in Bessie's diary noted the rumoured evacuation of all school children in the town of Kirkwall and the eventual evacuation of all women and children from throughout the Orkneys.

In her diary entry for the following day, Bessie wrote that she had attended her Guild meeting, where there was much discussion among the members regarding evacuation plans. These plans, she later learned, were proven to be false. In her final comments that evening, Bessie wrote of the sinking of a British tanker at nearby Inganess Bay.

A short time later, as the air war increased over the islands, additional anti-aircraft batteries were installed on the neighbouring island of Shapinsay, along with more than one hundred men and officers to operate them.

On the last day of January 1940, three ships were sunk near Scapa Flow, where thousands of men and women were now stationed at the Naval Base. Two of the vessels were destroyers, the third was a coast guard patrol boat. Many lives were lost. One body from the sinkings was found on the beach near Sandgarth.

That same day, Bessie wrote that she continued to discover fragments of wood along the shore, and that new anti-aircraft installations would be arriving in Stromberry, along with a searchlight.

Less than a week later, three more bodies were washed ashore, and a single German plane fired on the ship, *Rota*, inflicting only slight damage. The aircraft then proceeded on to the neighbouring island of Shapinsay, bombing an armed trawler. Coast guard patrols moved in to defend the trawler as the plane circled and finally flew off.

On 10 February, Bessie found a hundred pound keg of Danish butter on the beach. The wood was water-soaked and fragile, but otherwise untouched. Walking a bit further, she spotted an empty cask. As Bessie was making her discoveries, two German submarines were sunk in nearby waters.

Several days later, one of the war's first mass rescues took place far to the north in a Norwegian fjord, when two hundred and ninety-nine British prisoners from HMS *Cossack* were taken from the German warship, *Altmark*, and brought to safety.

On the evening of 16 March, while Bessie was shopping in the village, the sounds of enemy aircraft approached. Running out of the store with a friend, Bessie counted no less than a dozen German fighters in a sky emblazoned with fire-power from both the aircraft and artillery guns from the British Fleet at Scapa Flow harbour. Suddenly, a tremendous flash broke out in the waters near Kirkwall, more than likely a ship under attack rather than the oil tanks or the aerodrome.

Then nine planes from the squadron broke away and headed for the northern area of the island where Kirkwall was located. From another direction came the roar of additional fighters.

During a momentary lull in the action, Bessie raced for home. As she reached the village of Newhouse, the firing intensified and the skies were lit by flashes of fire from Stromness, 'lighting up the west Mainland hills brilliantly', as Bessie recorded in her diary. Sixteen searchlights swept through the darkness as anti-aircraft shells blasted overhead. The smell of gunpowder choked the air and shrapnel fell from every direction as Bessie finally reached her farmhouse. Soon, the planes moved off into the distance and all was quiet.

In her diary on the following day, Bessie described in depth the bombing of the Scapa Flow Naval Base and the blowing up of the Bridge of Waithe. In that action, a battleship was hit, as well as seven cottages in the village of Stenness. Seven people were injured and one life had been lost. All-out war had come to the Orkneys. On his regular broadcast over the radio later that evening, the Nazi sympathizer known as Lord Haw Haw revelled in the damage that had been inflicted on the islands, reporting that the German raids had been successful and that none of the country's planes had been lost.

Bessie concluded her report by suggesting that there had been much initial confusion as the raid got underway, and there were rumours that the pilots were young and newly trained . . .

Enemy action in the waters surrounding the islands was on the increase. Bessie wrote of an attack on a British convoy, and the damaging of three destroyers. A fourth had to be scuttled.

Despite all of the events that were unfolding, life on Mainland continued. Bessie excitedly described the dress rehearsal for the village concert, and of one participant's difficulty in speaking plainly enough to be heard. Another in the group caught the measles and had to be replaced . . . a dance had been scheduled and a number of the newly arrived Territorials (soldiers of the volunteer reserve forces) were expected to attend . . . a friend had gone to the village of Stromness to see the houses that had been bombed . . . the Bridge of Waithe was salvageable . . . the concert was a success and Bessie's recitation 'good'.

On 25 March, the Territorials installed a searchlight at the Elwickbank Park and additional anti-aircraft guns. The lorry carrying the machinery passed Bessie's farm. As they moved down the road, the soldiers aboard the convoy waved cheerfully at Bessie and she waved back. Her mother showed her displeasure at this behaviour by not allowing her to attend a dance the men gave shortly after.

Two days after the report about the arrival of the equipment, Bessie found out that the large object she had seen on the lorry was an anti-aircraft detector, 'the very latest device'.

Bessie also noted that Miss Balfour, the spinster who lived in the nearby castle, had issued orders that the Territorials billeted with her would not be permitted to take their meals inside, so the soldiers had to set up their stoves on the tennis court and 'eat there in the rain'! In addition, they were to remove their boots before entering the building. Their lieutenant, however, was served his meals inside.

In this same entry, Bessie described the anticipated arrival of fifty Gordons from Lancashire, and went on to say that Orcadians had difficulty understanding the men's accents, and the Gordons couldn't cope with the Orcadian dialect. So everyone would speak English . . .

That evening, Bessie wrote once again. Another German air raid come as dusk was falling. Tracer bullets scanned the skies overhead and searchlights on the islands of Shapinsay and Mainland shot upward, moving swiftly across the heavens as the aircraft approached. Suddenly, there was a tremendous thunder of firepower as the countryside was illuminated by shells and bullets exploding, and guns from the batteries sent brilliant flashes into the air. At one time, Bessie counted thirty-seven searchlight beams. As the action continued, she shouted encouragement, marching around excitedly and whistling 'Run, rabbit, run!'. This bravery she attributed to her Viking ancestry . . .

On 8 April, the British destroyer *Glowworm* was sunk off Norway after colliding with a German cruiser. Several days later, Germany invaded Denmark and landed in five strategic Norwegian cities.

The next day, Bessie noted that two German planes had been shot down and a third wouldn't 'get home'. While German soldiers paraded in the streets of Denmark, one hundred of their ships, including armed trawlers, minesweepers and battleships sailed for Norway.

At eight thirty that same night, the skies above Bessie's village were alive once again with firepower.

Kirkwall was also under attack, and as air raid sirens sounded their warning, searchlights above all of the surrounding villages went to work. As Bessie and her family watched, the lights centred on a huge aircraft, a four-engine bomber, roaring overhead with its tail-guns firing. In the bay below the village, an armed trawler fired back in defence. Soon after, Bessie lost sight of the plane. In her diary that night, she wrote that at the height of the raid, as bullets and shells flashed all about, 'the lapwings were crying, and above it all, a pale crescent moon looked down. It was weirdly beautiful.'

On 10 May, as the Germans invaded The Netherlands, Belgium, Luxembourg and France, Churchill replaced the ineffective Chamberlain as Prime Minister. Bessie reported the dropping of hundreds of enemy parachutes over Holland and Belgium, and expressed her dismay that all of Norway with the exception of the port at Narvik had been lost.

Several days later, an officer from the searchlight battery patrol spotted an enemy submarine cruising through the bay at Scapa Flow during the night. German planes carrying parachutists ready for a jump over Mainland had been intercepted by British fighters in hot pursuit. Following this action, the Territorials strengthened their defences.

On 20 May, Winston Churchill delivered the first of many brilliant addresses which served to inspire hope in the hearts and minds of the British people:

*I speak to you for the first time as Prime Minister
in a solemn hour for the life of our country, of our
Empire, of our Allies, and above all, of the cause
of Freedom . . .*

In her diary that evening, Bessie noted, 'the war
gets more serious . . . I can hear heavy firing in the
east, but cannot see anything.' At the moment of her
writing, the Germans had captured the historic cities
of Abbeville and Amiens and were pushing towards
the English Channel at Noyelles.

In the entry which followed, Bessie mentioned
several 'very vivid dreams' that she had had during
the previous night. In each, she saw 'quarries and
water'. Later that day, 'a case of suicide or accidental
drowning occurred in Sands'.

Bessie Shea's final diary recording was made on 25
May 1940. In it, she reported that the Germans had
broken through the French lines of defence and
had captured Boulogne. 'I didn't hear the nine
o'clock news last night but the news is getting worse
and worse. What if Hitler wins? He *can't*. In all
human reason he can't.'

In the weeks to come, Hitler's forces penetrated
deep into the heart of France, until the British
Expeditionary Forces and their Allies had retreated
to the coast at Dunkirk, where, between 26 May and
4 June, the massive evacuation of 338,226 men took
place. On that day, a defiant Winston Churchill
addressed the House of Commons:

We shall go on to the end. We shall fight in France, we shall fight on the seas and oceans ... we shall fight on the landing grounds, we shall fight in the fields and in the streets, we shall fight in the hills; we shall never surrender ...

During the months that followed, the war steadily worsened. On 1 July, 217 merchant ships were sunk by German submarines in an effort to take control of the Atlantic, and on 10 July the first heavy bombing of British and Welsh docks took place, marking the beginning of the Battle of Britain.

By late August, the first bombs fell on central London, and on 1 September, the London Blitz had begun in earnest.

In the months and years that lay ahead Adolf Hitler scored victory after victory, and it appeared possible that Bessie Shea's worst fears would be realized and that Hitler would win. But that was not to be: Great Britain remained uninvaded for the duration of the war.

5
Endless Night

Tucked into the mountains of Romania, there is a peaceful little town called Sighet. In the surrounding countryside rivers and streams wind in and out of ancient hamlets where peasants tend their fields much as they have done for centuries. With the coming of spring, the air is filled with the freshness of the season and gardens come to life in a blaze of colour.

Here in Sighet, a young boy named Elie Wiesel once lived with his parents and three sisters. Elie's father was a merchant and a leader of the predominantly Jewish community. His mother was a well-educated woman whose life was centred around the teachings of the Hebrew scriptures.

Elie Wiesel was a serious child with a thirst for learning. At an early age, he began studying the

Torah and immersed himself in the rituals and prayers of the Hasidic faith. Unlike other boys in his neighbourhood, he preferred the synagogue to the playground.

On holy days, Elie's grandfather, Dodye Feig, visited the family for the ceremonial feasts and the services at the synagogue. Elie loved these visits because his grandfather was a remarkable storyteller who brought to life the ancient Hebrew legends.

In the little town of Sighet, the seasons came and went in undisturbed serenity, and the people remained untouched by the clouds of war that hung over much of Europe. And then, suddenly, everything changed.

In 1942, the Hungarian police who were in charge of Sighet and its neighbouring communities ordered the arrest and deportation of all foreign Jews. Among those was a wise little man known to everyone as Moshe the Beadle.

Elie Wiesel loved Moshe the Beadle, for it was he who had introduced him to the great books of the Hebrew scholars called the cabbala, which sought to explain the mysteries of the Hebrew teachings.

On the day of the deportation, the people of Sighet followed Moshe and the other foreign Jews to the train station. Carrying sacks of food, they presented them to their departing neighbours and wept as the people were herded into cattle trucks for unknown destinations. Elie watched as the trains left the station and he, too, wept.

Months passed and life in Sighet returned to

normal. In the market-place, food was plentiful, and in the streets the children played.

And then one evening as Elie was about to enter the synagogue, he saw Moshe the Beadle. Elie was stunned by the man's appearance and by the story he had to tell.

As the train carrying Moshe and the others crossed the Hungarian border and moved into German-occupied Polish territory, the Gestapo secret police boarded the trucks and ordered everyone out. Near the station platform, a long line of open trucks awaited the prisoners. Shouting at the people and pushing them along with their rifle butts, the Gestapo shoved the prisoners into the trucks and drove them into a dense forest.

Finally, the trucks stopped and again the people were ordered to get out. Brandishing their rifles, the Gestapo tossed shovels at the crowd and told them to dig. For hours the people struggled with their work. When they had finished, the soldiers started firing. Again and again, the shots rang through the forest as the people fell into the mass grave that they themselves had dug. Moshe was wounded in the leg and fell with the others, praying that the soldiers would believe him dead.

For a long time, Moshe lay quietly amidst the bodies that had fallen around and on top of him. Then, when the last truck had left the site of the slaughter, he climbed out of the ditch and hobbled slowly through the trees, leaving behind him his family, his children and his friends.

Why, Elie asked, had Moshe the Beadle returned to Sighet?

To warn the people, the little man answered. Terrible things were happening and the citizens of Sighet were no longer safe.

Day after day, Moshe the Beadle told his story of the massacre in the forest. He spoke to men and women in the factories and the synagogues and even in the market-place. But the people refused to listen. Nothing like that could possibly have happened. Poor old Moshe had gone mad.

In the evenings, the people gathered around their radios to listen to the news from London. In Germany, British and American war planes were targeting major cities and blowing up munitions works. Hitler had lost Stalingrad. There was even talk of a major offensive. Soon, the people said, it would all be over.

By the middle of 1943, the hard-fought campaign in north Africa was drawing to a close. By May, General Rommel, 'The Desert Fox', and his German forces had surrendered.

In April of the following year, as the warmth of spring returned to Sighet and the trees were bursting with buds, the Germans marched into Hungary. Three days later, German soldiers swept through the streets of Sighet.

At first, little happened. German officers established themselves in hotels and homes throughout the town. They ate in the coffee shops, shopped in the stores and bought fruit in the market-place. No shots were fired. No one was threatened. And the Jews of Sighet continued to believe that no harm would come to them.

With the approach of Passover week, the people busied themselves with their preparations. Houses were cleaned from top to bottom. Fresh curtains were hung at the windows and books were taken outdoors for a dusting. The women prepared the traditional foods for the Seder and the men gathered in prayer in their homes since orders had been issued for the closing of the synagogues.

During the week-long festivities, the people ate and drank and gave thanks that they had been spared.

On the seventh day of Passover, the leaders of the Jewish community were arrested by the Germans and all of the others were forbidden to leave their homes for three days. Anyone who did so would be shot. In addition, all gold and jewellery was to be turned over to the police.

Next, came the orders that all Jews were to wear a yellow star on their clothing. The people could no longer eat in restaurants, use public transport, or leave their homes after the curfew at six in the evening.

Shortly after, the Germans blocked off two sections of the town and established ghettos where all of the Jews of Sighet were to be confined. Since Elie's home was inside one of these sections, he and his family were not required to move like most of the other Jews in Sighet. But because the home was located on one of the corners of the new ghetto, all windows facing the outside street were sealed. Relatives who had been driven from their homes in other parts of the town moved in with the Wiesels. Each of the two ghettos was ringed by barbed wire.

For a time, the people felt safe. And for the next few weeks, the situation remained quiet. Elie and some of the other boys took their studies of the Talmud to a little park where they worked in the warmth of the spring sun.

Then one evening, just as dusk was falling, a man came into the courtyard where Elie and his father and a few others had gathered. Something was happening. The Gestapo had been seen patrolling the ghetto, and a special meeting of the Jewish Council had been called. Elie's father, a member of the council, left immediately with the messenger.

As the hours dragged by, people in the ghetto crowded into the courtyard. At midnight, Elie's father returned with the dreaded news. Both ghettos in Sighet were to be liquidated and the people deported. Each person would be permitted to take a sack of clothing and food enough to last for the journey. The people listened in silence.

Later that night, one of Elie's relatives in the house rushed into the room where he and his parents and sisters were trying to sleep. Someone had been heard knocking on one of the windows that faced the outside of the ghetto. A warning, perhaps? A Christian offering a place to hide? But by the time everyone reached the window, the person had fled.

At dawn the next day, Elie and his family buried

what they could of the family treasures: his mother, the silver candelabra that she used on the eve of Shabbat each week; his father, the savings of a lifetime. Elie's older sisters buried what things they could near the cellar; Elie and his younger sister, Tzipora, worked in the garden under a tall poplar tree. Elie buried the gold watch he had been given less than two years before in honour of his Bar Mitzvah. Tzipora hid a favourite toy.

By eight o'clock in the morning, the police were swarming in the streets, banging on doors and shouting to the people to empty their houses. Soon, everyone was standing outside with their sacks of clothing and food.

Elie watched as the first groups of people were led away. Behind them in the streets lay all of the things they had not been allowed to take with them: family portraits, suitcases, eating utensils and other remnants of their once normal lives.

Elie and his family, along with several others, were ordered to march to the second of the two ghettos. Elie cast a backward glance at the home that had been his since birth. In it, he had prayed and fasted and studied. In it, he had felt the love and security of his family. And then he heard his father, weeping.

Elie's mother walked silently in front of him. His seven-year-old sister Tzipora struggled under the weight of her sack. All around them, the police were shouting to the people to run. Old men and women, the sick and the very young were beaten with clubs as they passed through the street.

When the people reached the second ghetto, they

were shocked by what they saw. Windows smashed, doors ajar, belongings scattered through the streets. Inside one of his relative's homes, Elie later discovered a bowl of unfinished soup and a pie ready for the oven. On the floor, a litter of books.

Each cattle truck held eighty people. One person in each truck was put in charge of the others. If anyone tried to escape, the person in charge would be shot. Loaves of bread and buckets of water were delivered to each car. The trucks were sealed up and the windows barred. And then, slowly, the train began to move.

Inside the trucks, the people stood shoulder to shoulder in the suffocating darkness. Since there was no room to lie down, each took turns sitting down. After days of travel, the water ran out and the people grew ill with thirst. And still the train moved on.

At last the train arrived at its destination: Auschwitz-Birkenau, one of the six extermination camps that the Germans had established.

The doors were opened and the people ordered on to the platform. At the command, each removed wedding rings, watches and any other gold that they still possessed. At a second command, the men and boys were ordered to march to the left, the women and girls to the right.

Elie held on to his father's hand. Searching the crowd for the sight of his mother and sisters, his eyes fell on them, walking with bowed heads in the opposite direction. As they walked, Elie's mother stroked his little sister's long, blonde hair.

The air was stifling and the people choked on the trail of acrid smoke that rose from tall chimmneys in the distance. On and on they marched.

The men and boys reached the centre of the square. At the front of the line stood the infamous Dr Mengele with baton in hand, ready for the 'first selection'. As each prisoner stepped up to be examined, the officer pointed his baton first in one direction and then the other. Those who looked healthy were marched off to the cell blocks. The ill, the elderly and the lame were sent to the gas chambers.

Elie and his father were among those to survive that first day. His mother and his little sister Tzipora were gassed.

On their way to the cell blocks, Elie and his father saw flames shooting up from a ditch. Trucks were unloading the bodies of little children and tossing them into the fires.

Once inside the cell blocks the prisoners were stripped of their clothing except for their shoes and belts. Heads were shaved and all body hair removed. And then the beatings began.

Before sunrise the next morning, Elie and the others, still naked but for their shoes, were taken to a second barracks where they were dipped in gasoline for disinfection and then marched into the showers. In still another building, they were issued clothing. A cap, a loose shirt, pants. Next came a second separation

71

as an SS officer ordered all skilled workers to march.

Elie and his father, along with those in the second group, were taken to another building. More beatings took place during which Elie saw his father struck to the ground. Then, after another march on the run, the prisoners came to the entrance of a second camp. SS troops surrounded them, brandishing machine guns as police dogs stood alert by their sides.

As the men and boys passed through another gate, they looked up at a huge sign that read, 'Work is Liberty!' They had arrived at Auschwitz.

Once again, the prisoners were ordered to remove their clothing and were taken into the showers. This was followed by endless hours of standing outside in the open air, clad only in their shoes. Dusk came and the skies grew dark as heavy smoke from the crematoria billowed above their heads. Finally, at midnight, the prisoners were assigned to a new barracks. Rows of wooden bunks stacked in tiers stretched down a long, dark room where the only light came from skylights high above. Two men were directed to each bunk. There were no mattresses.

On the following day, Elie and the others were given new uniforms. That afternoon, each prisoner stood in line to receive a tattoo on the left arm. With this final humiliation, each had been reduced to a nameless number.

Three weeks later, after walking for four hours through the German countryside, the new prisoners arrived at a third concentration camp called Buna.

Here, Elie and the others were given medical examinations, after which their teeth were checked by a line of dentists. On their note pads, the dentists recorded a mark beside the number of each prisoner who had gold crowns or fillings in his mouth. Gold was valuable to the Germans. Elie had one gold crown.

When the examinations had been completed, each of the prisoners was given his work orders and Elie was assigned to an electrical equipment warehouse.

One day while Elie was working in the warehouse, a guard came towards him and began beating him. Then the guard threw his entire weight on the boy and continued to beat his head, face and body. Elie took each blow in silence, knowing that if he cried out he could be killed.

At last, the beating stopped and the guard moved away. Elie crawled back to where he had been working. Leaning against the wall for a moment, he closed his eyes as the pain from the beating ran through his body. Soon, he felt a gentle hand wiping the blood from his face. Elie looked up to see a young girl smiling faintly at him. Then, pushing a small crust of bread into his hand, the girl whispered a few comforting words and went quietly back to her work place.

One day, the leader of Elie's labour gang threatened to take out his gold crown. The boy told him that one of the dentists had already noted the crown on their record sheets. If the gang leader stole the crown without the dentists' knowledge, he could get into trouble. The gang leader laughed and made it clear that it would be Elie who would get into trouble if he didn't obey orders.

When Elie's father heard what had happened, he told his son that he must not give into the gang leader's intimidation. Elie argued that if he refused to respond to the threats, it could be dangerous for both of them.

Several days later, Elie's warning came true when the gang leader discovered that his father could not march in step as the prisoners moved from one place to another in the camp. Each time Elie's father broke the rhythm of the compulsory beat, the gang leader hit him with his club.

Weeks went by, and the clubbings continued. Finally, Elie could stand it no more, and begged his father to let him give in to the bully. The gold crown was removed with a rusty spoon.

As the months passed, the Allies stepped up their bombing raids over Germany. Frequently, Elie and the others heard the distant thumps of anti-aircraft guns, and on most nights, squadrons of American and British planes could be seen flying back to their bases in England.

On a Sunday morning late in 1944, when Elie's half of the prisoners were in their barracks and the others were at work in their labour gangs, Buna's air raid sirens sounded. Immediately, all of the guards in the watch towers left their posts and raced for the shelters. SS troops took up their stations throughout the camp to shoot any prisoners who tried to escape during the air raid.

As the sirens continued to wail, a man crept out from one of the buildings and slowly crawled towards two large soup cauldrons that had been set up outside for the noon ration. As yet unnoticed by the guards, the prisoner inched towards the cauldrons. Reaching the first of the two cauldrons, he struggled to lift himself upwards towards the opening in the top. Suddenly, the roar of machine guns exploded in the air and the prisoner fell back to the ground.

Soon, the drone of airplanes was heard overhead, and as Elie listened, bombs began to rain down on the camp. Buildings trembled and the skylights in Elie's barracks rattled with the barrage. Buna was under attack. The prisoners shouted to one another. Would the Allies rescue them today?

After an hour, the bombings ceased. Outside, all was quiet. At last, the sirens sounded the all-clear.

As the air raids increased and the Germans continued to be beaten back throughout Europe, Nazi retaliation against the tens of thousands of prisoners at the Buna camp grew more frequent. Hangings became common practice, and at each, the prisoners were forced to witness the final agony. Food rations dwindled and the men and boys grew weak with hunger.

September came, and with it, Rosh Hashanah, the holy day that observed the passing of the Jewish calendar year. On the evening before, all of the prisoners who were able to walk gathered together on the grounds outside their barracks. The solemn prayers were uttered, first by the officiant, and then by the thousands of men and boys who had crowded into the area. Elie heard the mournful chants as each prayer was offered. With each response came the anguished cries of a desolate people. The voice of the officiant grew faint as he choked on his words. At the end of the service the prisoners uttered the Kaddish – the Hebrew prayer for the dead – in memory of lost parents, children, sisters and brothers and friends.

Elie and his father were separated from one another. Elie was moved to a new barracks and assigned to a new labour gang. For twelve hours each day, he dragged and lifted building blocks heavier than his own small frame. Beside him, worked a man who had once been a Rosh-Yeshiva, a teacher of the Hebrew scriptures.

Soon after Elie's arrival, the prisoner spoke to him. Whatever the cost, the young boy must not give in to the evil that surrounded him. He must keep his mind alert in order to preserve his soul. In order to do so, one must study.

Day after day, Elie and the prisoner recited the scriptures together. As they worked, the pages of the Torah slowly crept into the young boy's mind and the years of study in the little town of Sighet came back to him. Eventually, Elie began to visualize the lines of the sacred scriptures, and felt himself growing stronger once again in spirit. And then one morning, the man was gone.

Elie's block leader, a Jew from Czechoslovakia, came into the barracks before mealtime one evening, announcing that two bowls of soup would be awarded to the prisoner who could tell the best story. Eager for the extra ration, one after another of the inmates responded.

Finally, the block leader came to Elie. After much urging, the young boy began to describe the meal that he had so often pictured in his mind – the Shabbat meal held each Friday in his home in Sighet. The starched white damask, the silver candelabra, his little sister Tzipora setting the special dishes on the table. The sacred songs and the blessing of the bread and wine. And grandfather seated among the others gathered for the meal. All around him, the prisoners listened with heads bowed. Each had shared in Elie's story. Each had broken the bread and sipped the wine. Throughout the barracks, a hushed silence prevailed. That evening, Elie Wiesel was awarded two bowls of soup.

Early one evening after the prisoners had returned from work, they were told not to go into the yards after the food ration had been handed out. A selection was about to take place, and the weakest of the prisoners would be sent to the gas chambers.

Later that night, as the prisoners stood naked by

their bunks, three SS officers came into the barracks followed by Dr Mengele, the Nazi officer who had greeted them all at Birkenau.

According to procedure, each prisoner was to run as fast as he could down the length of the aisle to the place where the officers stood. There, the colour of the prisoner's skin was checked, the arms and legs tested for strength and the eyes examined for alertness. With notebook in hand, Mengele made a mark here and there beside a prisoner's number. Finally, it was Elie's turn.

With all the strength he could muster, Elie ran down the aisle past the prisoners standing at attention. Would tonight be the night he would be taken? Facing Dr Mengele, Elie's mind raced as the colour of his skin was examined, and then his arms and legs and eyes. At last the order came for him to return to his bunk. Had they seen the number on his arm? He had tried to hide it so that they wouldn't know who he was.

Elie was not chosen for the furnaces that night. But others were . . .

Early one morning while Elie was standing in line waiting for his labour gang to march to the building site, his father came to tell him that the time had finally come: he had been one of those who had been selected. With eyes tormented by fear and hunger, Elie's father reached under his shirt and brought out his eating utensils. Someday, Elie could trade them if he had to for a piece of bread.

When the order came for Elie's group to march, he saw his father walk to the wall of a building and lean against it. Suddenly, Elie's father started running towards the group. But it was too late. The group had passed through the gate.

Throughout the day, Elie performed his duties at the building site as though he were in a trance. Knowing of his anguish, several of the workers tried to assure him that his father would be relieved of his sentence.

Returning to the camp later that day, Elie ran to his father's barracks. Moving down the aisle to his father's bunk, he could scarcely believe his eyes. There, on the bunk before him, sat his father! He had convinced the officers that he could still work, and therefore, was still useful. Elie and his father held on to one another for a brief moment. And then, reaching into his shirt, he brought out his father's eating utensils and handed them back to him.

With the arrival of winter, the days grew short and the nights bitter and cold. Elie and the other prisoners felt the wind whipping through their shirts as their bare hands struggled with the building stones. Rumours spread that the Germans were losing on all fronts and that the war would soon be over. Elie could not allow himself to think of such a miracle.

And then the word came. Buna was to be liquidated and the prisoners would be taken to another concentration camp called Buchenwald. Those who were ill or too weak to walk would be left behind.

On the night that the news had broken, Elie walked through the snow to his father's barracks. Whatever happened now, they must not be separated. Elie wondered if his father were strong enough for the journey. Would he be able to keep up with the others?

Together, the father and son spoke of their concerns and of the certainty that those who remained in Buna would be exterminated. Most likely, the camp itself would be blown up to destroy all evidence of what had taken place there. In the end, the two decided that they stood a greater chance of survival by marching to Buchenwald.

That night, as Elie lay in his bunk, the skylights above him rattled with the vibrations of distant gunfire. The Russians were advancing.

In the morning, the prisoners were given an extra ration of bread. In the storage rooms, the guards allowed them to take whatever items of clothing they could fit over their uniforms. Blankets would serve as coats.

By nightfall, all was ready. Searchlights blazed through the darkness, illuminating tens of thousands of prisoners as they lined up in formation. Wrapping their blankets tightly about them, they waited silently in the falling snow for the units ahead of them to move. At last, Elie's unit heard the order to march.

Surrounded by SS officers and their dogs, the prisoners marched through the countryside. Wind whipped about them in sudden gusts, and snow bit into their faces. From every direction, the officers shouted at them to move faster and faster until, finally, they were running. Through village after village the prisoners ran until those who could no longer keep up fell behind. Some of them dropped down into the snow and were trampled to death. In the confusion, Elie managed to find his father.

Numbness set in and with it the desire to let oneself go, to give up and to fall with the others. Because of his father, Elie knew that he must go on. He must take care of his father, running alongside him, weaker now and short of breath.

On and on through the night the prisoners ran, twenty miles, twenty-five, thirty and more. An endless procession moving in silence as the bodies of the fallen bloodied the snow. Elie felt himself pushed along by the mob. To stop now meant death.

At dawn, the order came to rest. Elie and his father took refuge in an abandoned factory along with a crowd of other prisoners. Each took turns at sleeping. They had covered more than forty-three miles.

The snow continued throughout the day while the prisoners rested. Elie and his father fought against the hunger and thirst that wracked their bodies. At dusk, they were on the move again, leaving behind the dead, the wounded and those who could no longer continue.

The march was less ordered now. Beside them, the prisoners heard the roar of motorcycles as SS officers shouted to them to press on. Soon they would arrive in Gleiwitz.

Passing through the barbed wire, Elie and his father

were ordered into a crowded barracks, stumbling over men who had dropped to the floor with exhaustion. For three days, they remained at Gleiwitz without food or water. As the hours passed, the thud of artillery guns grew closer and closer.

On the final day, the prisoners were given a small ration of bread and ordered into open cattle trucks. SS troops moved up and down the train platform with their dogs, shouting orders. The last stage of the journey to Buchenwald had begun.

For ten days, the train pushed through the countryside, past villages and farmlands. The snow continued to fall, covering the prisoners huddled in their blankets. Each morning, the train stopped and those who had died during the night were taken away.

On the evening of the tenth day, the train arrived in Buchenwald. At the beginning of the journey, one hundred prisoners had been crammed into each of the cattle trucks. In Elie's, only twelve had survived.

In the morning, Elie's father, struck down by hunger and fever, was taken to a barracks with other sick prisoners. Elie took him something to drink and spoke what words of comfort he could.

Days passed and Elie's father grew weak with dysentery. Prisoners in bunks to either side stole his rations of bread and struck out at him because he could no longer go to the lavatory. Desperate and unable to get any help, Elie moved into the barracks and found an empty bunk above his father's. Here, he would be able to watch over him.

One week later, on 29 January 1945, Mr Wiesel died.

For the next four months, Elie moved about, seeing nothing, feeling nothing. He had lost his mother, his little sister and his father. Of his two older sisters, he had had no news. Life was empty of meaning. Transferred to the children's block with six hundred others, he spent the days lying on his bunk, staring into space.

On 11 April, the Americans arrived. Elie and the other children in his barracks listened as the first of the tanks rolled into the camp. The tanks stopped and the soldiers got out. Silence descended as the men walked up and down the yards, unable to believe what they saw. The emaciated prisoners, the crematoria and everywhere on the ground, the skeletal bodies of dead prisoners.

Soldiers came into Elie's barracks, their faces contorted, tears running down their cheeks. As they moved down the rows of bunks, some of the men gave way to sobs of anger and rage.

One day, Elie, like Nechama Bawnik, Karla Poewe and others, would write of his experiences. In 1986, he was awarded the Nobel Peace Prize for his memoir of the Holocaust, *Night*.

Today, as a writer, teacher and lecturer, Elie Wiesel works tirelessly for the cause of human rights throughout the world. Addressing what he considers to be the moral obligation of people everywhere to protect the welfare and rights of others, he writes:

> *There is so much to be done, there is so much that can be done ... one person of integrity can make a difference, a difference between life and death.*

6
The Silent Rescuer

One thousand years ago, Vikings in their dragon-like longboats sailed out of the northern seas to attack and plunder lands along the western coast of Europe, moving south into the Mediterranean and finally westward across the sea to Iceland, Greenland and Newfoundland. At various points along the north-western coast of France, they navigated through rivers that led inland from the sea with such force that the King of France gave in to their might and offered them an area of land that had been so violently sacked he considered it no longer valuable.

The Vikings accepted the proposal, settled in and conferred upon their chieftain the title of Duke of the Norsemen. Later, the area became known as Normandy.

The province of Normandy is one of the most beautiful in France. The lush countryside is dense with forests and hedgerows and the rich soil produces some of the finest fruits and vegetables in the country. Along the area of the coastline facing the English Channel, cattle and sheep graze in the marshlands. In the offshore waters, fishermen cast their nets for delicate sole, or move on to the North Sea for an abundance of herring and cod.

The people of Normandy are a rugged and sturdy lot, proud of the land that produced their noble ancestor known as William, the Duke of Normandy, conqueror of all of Britain.

By October 1940, the province of Normandy was occupied by the Germans. And in a little coastal village near Caen, the people practised a quiet resistance, casting their eyes upward whenever they passed a group of German soldiers. One of those who followed this custom was a young schoolboy named Pierre.

The three hundred inhabitants of Pierre's village were aware of the fact that their location near the coast was of great value to the Germans. A network of nearby railways, rivers and canals would soon turn the region into a strategic centre for the mobilization of troops and military supplies. Now, with the Occupation, the once jovial people of the little village were solemn and filled with contempt for their invaders.

One morning, as German troops on motorcycles roared down the streets of the village, Henri Duplay, the beloved old schoolmaster who had taught the area's children for more than forty years, trudged along the narrow passageway that led to his school. Badly in need of repair, the building leaned up against an ancient church which, like the schoolhouse, had been heavily damaged by air raids.

Along the route, Monsieur Duplay's friend Renaud, the chemist, called a grave *bonjour* to him. Paul Marcellin, the local butcher, took down his shutters, shrugging over the futility of keeping open a shop that had nothing to sell. Outside the bakery further down the street, a long queue awaited the possibility that a loaf of bread might serve to expand the meagre offering of the evening's meal. As in all the other occupied countries, the food was controlled by the Germans and was in short supply.

On that particular morning, Monsieur Duplay was weary from lack of sleep. As he walked along, he wondered if it would not be wise to give up his work at the schoolhouse and join the Free French and their leader, General Charles de Gaulle, in London. There was so much to be done.

But what would become of his classes if he left? The school's only other teacher, Mademoiselle Martin, was tired and overworked as it was. And then, of course, there were his compatriots in the Resistance who needed his advice and who relied upon his judgment.

Reaching the school, Monsieur Duplay climbed the steps and plodded down the hallway to his classroom.

'*Bonjour, maître*,' the children called out in quiet unison.

'*Bonjour, mes enfants*,' the old schoolmaster replied warmly.

Later that day, as the children tumbled out of the schoolhouse and charged through the iron gate that led to the street, Pierre Labiche followed silently behind the rest. He preferred to walk alone, in order to avoid the taunts of four of his classmates. The leader of the group, Jacques Fournier, had earned a reputation as the bully of the playground, and although Pierre had no fear of the boy he wisely kept his distance.

A mute from birth, Pierre Labiche could neither speak nor hear. Despite these handicaps, however, he was able to communicate remarkably, having developed a sign language of his own that enabled him to continue his studies and to 'speak' to his friends and teachers. Pierre had other attributes as well. With his keen mind and ready smile, he was known and loved by everyone in the village.

Pierre's mother had died when he was an infant and his father, an army reservist, had been killed earlier in the war in the Maginot Line. For some time the boy had lived with his Aunt Paulette in a tiny thatched cottage just outside the village, facing the sea. To the rear of the half timbered building was an old apple orchard and a small vegetable garden. A densely wooded area lay beyond.

As Pierre made his way down the street, the four

88

boys ahead of him turned around and shouted one last insult.

With that, Monsieur Renaud appeared at the doorway of his pharmacy to witness the daily ridiculing. Shaking his head, he called to Pierre and motioned to him to come into the shop. The two shook hands and the boy flashed his familiar smile as he accepted a small packet of peppermint tea for Aunt Paulette. Then, from behind the counter, he scribbled a note on a scrap of paper and showed it to Pierre, who quickly read the words, 'Tonight, 1.30.' The child acknowledged the message and watched as Monsieur Renaud destroyed the paper with his lighted cigarette.

When Pierre arrived home, he found his aunt working in her vegetable garden. Although the German Command had ordered her to turn over all that she grew, she managed to smuggle a lot of her produce to her neighbours and to keep enough for Pierre and herself.

'What the eye doesn't see,' Paulette would say to friends who were well aware of her hatred of the enemy. The old woman had lost all of the men in her family to the Germans in three wars – two of them in her own lifetime.

Pierre communicated Monsieur Renaud's message to his aunt, whose hands quickly signed a warning: 'Be careful, Pierre, you are now the only man in the family, and our family must live on for France!'

That night, Pierre knelt by his bedroom window,

staring out through the darkness that enveloped the village each night after the curfew had sounded. Not a light could be seen anywhere. Pierre's eyes searched the cloud-covered skies for aircraft. Since he could not hear, he had developed an extraordinary ability to see things others could not.

As his aunt came into the room to bid him goodnight, Pierre suddenly saw the flash of German anti-aircraft fire. In an instant, the sky was flooded with searchlights and Aunt Paulette signalled to him that she could hear a plane approaching.

A minute later, Pierre thought he saw something white floating down from the sky. Could it be a parachute? The boy's mind raced as he quickly threw on his clothes and gestured to his aunt. Despite the curfew, he was going to find out if he had been right about what he thought he had seen.

In the silence of the woods behind Pierre's cottage, an American airman flying with the RAF released himself from his parachute and folded it quickly as he looked around for a place to bury it. Then, from somewhere close by, he heard something. Turning in the direction of the sound, the airman waited. Seconds passed as he reached for his revolver and switched on his pocket torch. Aiming it cautiously at the ground immediately in front of him, he spotted Pierre a few feet away. As the officer moved towards him, the boy put his finger to his lips to warn him not to talk.

Ripping a knife from his jacket, Pierre motioned toward the airman's parachute and crept to a spot where it could be buried. Then, slashing the officer's equipment into several pieces, he dug a shallow hole, filled it with the shreds and covered them with tree branches. As he was doing so, the airman asked Pierre who he was. The boy responded with a smile, grabbing his hand and leading him silently through the woods toward a neighbour's farm.

As the two emerged from the trees, they heard the sounds of dogs barking. Pierre dropped into a ditch behind the farmhouse and pulled the officer down with him. As the officer lay beside the boy, bombs exploded in the distance. The RAF was doing its work.

Glancing at the child beside him in the ditch, the airman wondered if he were right in following him. He decided to take his chances.

After a few minutes, the barking ceased and the boy motioned to the officer to crawl along beside him, as he dodged between trees and finally behind the hedgerows that led to his cottage.

Once again Pierre came to a stop, signalling to the officer to lie down. In the distance, he had spotted a faint light moving slowly through the black of the night. A second later, the airman heard a car approaching. Suddenly, a searchlight shot through the area and the two hid their faces as the beam swept over their heads.

The car inched closer and then came to a stop a few yards away. Two German officers got out of the car. As they stood talking, the pilot listened to their voices, understanding enough of the language to pick up their conversation.

One of the officers said he doubted that anyone

could have survived the impact of the explosion on the plane that was hit. And if so, the pilot would have landed closer to the city of Caen.

The second officer was restless and wanted to get back into the protection of the car. These Frenchmen in the Resistance would stop at nothing to stab a German. And besides, he'd had enough riding around and was ready for a decent glass of Calvados.

As the Germans drove off, the airman glanced at the boy once again. His hunch had been right. The child was trying to protect him.

Silence returned, and the two resumed their journey, crawling through the thick brush of the hedgerows.

After a short distance, Pierre halted and pointed to the pilot's luminous wristwatch, holding up two fingers and nodding his head. Then he crept away. Seconds later, the officer heard the sound of pebbles striking a window pane.

Flight Officer Elmer Tracy found himself standing in a woodshed behind Aunt Paulette's cottage. Having introduced himself as an American who had volunteered for the RAF, he acknowledged that he could speak some French and could understand the language quite well. Then he asked about the unusual child who had rescued him.

He was her nephew, the old woman answered, explaining that they communicated with one another through sign language because the boy was mute.

The officer, concerned about his former doubts about the boy, apologized. But wasn't Pierre too young to take such risks?

Aunt Paulette's answer was simple: one was never too old nor to young to fight for one's country's freedom.

Moving quickly about the shed, the woman reached into a box and withdrew a shabby old suit. Handing it to the officer, she asked that he put it on and then give her his uniform. At first, the man protested. Did these people know what danger they were in? If the Germans found out . . .

After the officer had changed into the suit, Aunt Paulette knelt on the floor of the woodshed and began removing a number of heavy logs. Then she pushed aside a dirt covering and removed several wooden planks to reveal an opening in the ground. A number of steps led to a small underground hiding place just large enough for a cot.

Again, the airman protested. It would be better for all of them if he left.

But Aunt Paulette would have none of it. Lieutenant Tracy was not the first airman she had hidden and he would not be the last: trust in God and the Resistance. Then, handing him a bottle of Calvados and a glass, she climbed the steps to the woodshed and whispered goodnight.

In class the next morning, Pierre was filled with fear. The teacher had not yet appeared and the students around him were restless. Pierre could think of only one thing. The Germans had learned of his teacher's activities in the Resistance and had come for him during the night. Pierre clung to the one positive thought in his mind. When he stopped at the pharmacy for the morning's messages nothing had been said about the schoolmaster.

Finally, Monsieur Duplay appeared. As Pierre breathed a sigh of relief, the schoolmaster explained that he had had a restless night and had overslept. Pierre smiled to himself, knowing the truth about his teacher's secret work.

Monsieur Duplay turned to the blackboard and wrote the name of one of France's greatest heroines, Charlotte Corday. Underneath the woman's name he wrote: 'She teaches us how to die.' Then, turning back to the children, he began the morning's discussion.

Suddenly, the classroom door burst open and in walked three German officers. One of the officers spoke. Reading the message on the blackboard aloud, he turned on Monsieur Duplay in a rage. What was the meaning of this trash? he demanded.

This was an important name in France's history, the old schoolmaster explained.

France no longer had a history, the officer shot back. The Germans would see to that. Then, turning to face the class, the officer addressed the students.

During the night, German anti-aircraft fire had hit an RAF plane, one of a squadron that was returning to its base in England after a raid. A single parachute had been spotted and the airman was believed to be hiding somewhere in the village. A reward of fifty thousand francs would be given to the student who could volunteer information that would lead to the capture of the airman.

For a time, none of the children spoke. The officer was furious, and threatened reprisals if someone didn't speak. Certain facts had surfaced. Among them was a report that a boy had been seen going into the woods near Madame Paulette's cottage.

Finally, Jacques Fournier spoke from the back of the room. The boy whom the authorities were looking for must be Pierre Labiche.

The students in the classroom were stunned. How could Jacques do such a thing to Pierre?

Ignoring his classmates, Jacques continued. On his way to school that morning, he had seen Pierre eating some chocolate. It must have been English chocolate, because no one in the village had seen that kind of delicacy since the Occupation had begun, Jacques said, pointing to the boy.

The officer walked over to where Pierre was sitting and asked him his name. Sensing that something was terribly wrong, Pierre looked first at the officer and then at Monsieur Duplay.

Getting no response, the German asked the question a second time, and again, there was silence. Infuriated, the officer struck Pierre across the face with his leather glove. In spite of the pain, the child didn't flinch.

Monsieur Duplay spoke. He tried to explain . . .

Quiet! the German ordered, turning on Pierre for the last time with his question. When Pierre couldn't respond, the officer struck him again with his glove.

As the children watched in horror, Gabrielle, the pharmacist's daughter, blurted out the fact that Pierre was a mute and could neither hear nor speak.

The officer demanded to know how the schoolmaster communicated with the boy.

By sign language, Monsieur Duplay answered.

Then find out where he was last night, the German said.

The schoolmaster flashed a warning to Pierre. Then he signalled to the boy to go to the blackboard and write that he had been at home with his aunt all evening and that the teacher had given him the chocolate the day before.

As Pierre did so, Monsieur Duplay opened a drawer in his desk and took out an old chocolate wrapper, reminding the officer that the Germans had given the candy to the schoolchildren on the day they had moved into the village.

With this, the officers gave up in frustration and after a final threat to the students and the schoolmaster, stormed out of the room.

Monsieur Duplay turned to Jacques Fournier, and in a low voice asked him why he had pointed the finger at Pierre.

As his classmates glared at him, Jacques responded by saying that Pierre wouldn't share his chocolate with him that morning.

After school that afternoon, Monsieur Duplay asked Pierre if he had anything to tell him.

Yes, the child answered in sign language. Aunt Paulette loved it when visitors came to the cottage.

Nodding his head in understanding, the schoolmaster warned Pierre to be careful. The Germans weren't entirely convinced of his innocence and would be watching for any careless slip-up. And then, as Pierre bid his teacher good day, Monsieur Duplay suggested that he would stop by that evening to write a 'letter' for his Aunt Paulette.

That evening at Madame Paulette's cottage, Monsieur Duplay memorized Flight Officer Tracy's identification card, going over the information repeatedly so that he could pass it along to the members of his Resistance group. That accomplished, he sat down at the kitchen table and wrote a letter which appeared to be meant for Madame Paulette's granddaughter in Alsace but was actually a coded message that Pierre would deliver at the appropriate time.

As the schoolmaster finished the letter, the sounds of motorcycles roared to a stop outside the cottage. Aunt Paulette ran to the cupboard and brought out an old puzzle for Pierre, handing it to him as a rifle butt banged on the door. Opening it, she stood back as two Germans, an officer and a sergeant, brushed past her.

As Pierre worked on his puzzle, the officer fired question after question at Aunt Paulette. What was her name?

Madame Labiche.

Who was the boy?

Pierre.

Who was the man?

A friend who was writing a letter for her because she was an uneducated woman and could not write.

What was in the letter? the officer demanded as he snatched the paper from the schoolmaster.

A letter to her only granddaughter, Aunt Paulette responded, telling her that the Germans in the village were treating the people with courtesy and had caused no harm to the citizens. The rest of the letter was filled with chatty news about affairs in the village.

Satisfied with the innocence of the letter, the German moved on to inspect the house, leaving the sergeant to guard Pierre and Monsieur Duplay.

Moving about the cottage, the officer resumed his questioning of Madame Paulette.

Noting the three small bedrooms, he went to several of the windows and looked out at the deep hedgerows and the secluded woods beyond the cottage. Suddenly, his eyes caught sight of the shed next to the vegetable garden.

What was in there? the German demanded.

Just an old woodshed, she replied, adding that he was welcome to go in, if he wouldn't mind the rats scurrying about his feet.

Turning from a window facing the woodshed, the officer announced that he would be leaving the sergeant at the cottage for a few days, since there was an extra bedroom. Madame Paulette gave her customary shrug and walked back into the kitchen.

Several evenings later, Monsieur Duplay, Monsieur Renaud and a number of other men and women gathered at the village inn for their weekly choir rehearsal, the single activity allowed by the Germans. As the practice got underway, Pierre served Calvados to the two officers who sat at a table, watching over the proceedings.

At the end of the rehearsal, everyone gathered at a table for a round of Calvados before the curfew sounded.

Pierre approached the table with his tray of brandy glasses. As he passed by the officers, one of them stuck out his boot and tripped the child, sending him to the floor with the tray.

Monsieur Renaud rushed to pick up Pierre and to help him with the tray and the shattered glasses as the owner of the inn began yelling at the boy in artificial disgust. Then, facing the schoolmaster, the owner told him to order Pierre to take the music and the practice accordian to the attic and put them in their usual place.

Quickly, Monsieur Duplay signalled the orders to Pierre, who immediately understood the message, picking up the music and the instrument. Running up the steps to the attic, he dropped everything in a corner and raced to the trap door in the roof of the attic. Tapping it softly, he opened the door, took Monsieur Duplay's folded 'letter' to Aunt Paulette's granddaughter from his mouth and shoved it into a basket that had been dropped from the roof.

Closing the trap door, Pierre returned to the room downstairs and continued to clean up the brandy and the glasses. While he was doing so, the story of Flight Officer Elmer Tracy was being transmitted by wireless radio to British headquarters in London.

Several days later in class, Gabrielle pushed a coded

note into Pierre's hand. Opening it, the boy read the words telling him that his aunt's 'medicine' was ready.

That afternoon after school, Pierre stopped at Monsieur Renaud's pharmacy. There, he picked up a bottle containing two capsules and a slip of paper giving directions for taking the medicine at eleven o'clock that night. The boy read the message and handed it back to the chemist who immediately set it ablaze with his cigarette.

At eleven o'clock that evening at the cottage, Pierre worked on his puzzle while his aunt did her mending and the sergeant wrote to his family in Germany.

Finishing her sewing, the old woman packed her things away, bid goodnight to Pierre and the sergeant, and left the room.

With this, the boy took his puzzle to the German and then went to a cask near the kitchen cupboard. There, he poured a large mug of cider from the cask and a small one for himself. During the time that the German had been billeted at the cottage, he had grown to like the strange little boy and had taken up the practice of helping him with his puzzle.

While they sat poring over the game, the Sergeant quickly emptied his mug of cider, commenting on its fine taste. At Pierre's invitation, the German had another one.

Before long, the sergeant began having difficulty piecing the puzzle together. Watching him closely, Pierre pretended not to notice the German's eyelids drooping and his words becoming slurred. Minutes later, the man lost consciousness and fell across the table. The 'two pills at eleven o'clock' had performed their duty.

After checking to make certain that the sergeant was indeed asleep, Madame Paulette hurried to the woodshed to tell Flight Officer Tracy that members of the Resistance would appear shortly to assist him in his escape.

Smiling appreciatively, the airman thanked the woman for all that she had done and asked to speak to Pierre before he left.

The woman shook her head, explaining that the child had to keep watch over the German in the kitchen.

With this, the American took off his wristwatch and handed it to Madame Paulette, asking her to give the watch to Pierre in gratitude for saving his life.

For a second time, the old woman refused the man's request, explaining that it would be dangerous to keep anything that would provide evidence of his having been hidden at the cottage. In the future, there would be others to rescue and more work to be done.

Minutes later, two men dressed in black fishermen's clothes rapped on the door of the woodshed. Madame Paulette whispered her blessings to the officer, and together the three men slipped into the darkness.

*

One morning less than a week after Flight Officer Tracy had left, Monsieur Duplay greeted his class and began the morning's lessons.

Glancing up from his book, he spotted the raised hand of Gabrielle Renaud, the pharmacist's daughter.

Monsieur Renaud had a question for the schoolmaster, the girl said. Could Monsieur Duplay explain to her father the words 'the future, the future, the future belongs to me' and whether or not they might have come from a poem?

The old schoolmaster put down his book, and after a brief sigh, responded by saying that the line had indeed been taken from a poem about Napoleon that the great French poet, Victor Hugo, had written many years before. With that, he signalled the message to Pierre.

Suddenly, a broad grin lit up the boy's face as he recognized the coded message. Officer Tracy had arrived safely in England.

Acknowledgements

The author gratefully acknowledges the permissions granted and courtesies extended for the use of background material from the following:

Bawnik, Nechama *Dry Tears: The Story of a Lost Childhood*, Nechama Bawnik Tec, New York, Oxford University Press (1984) for the Nechama Bawnik story

Cowan, Lore *Children of the Resistance: The Young Ones Who Defied the Nazi Terror*, Frewin, London (1968) for the Pierre Labiche story

Gollomb and Taylor *Young Heroes of the War*, The Vanguard Press, New York, (1943) for the Peter Brouet story

Poewe, Karla *Children in Germany During World War II* Edwin Mellen Press (1988) New York

Westall Robert *Children of the Blitz* Macmillan, London (1995) for the Bessie Shea story

Wiesel, Elie *Night*, Farrar, Straus and Giroux, New York (1982), original French edition published by Les Editions de Minuit, Paris (1958), Bantam Books, New York (1982)

Every effort has been made to trace copyright holders. We would be grateful to hear from any copyright holders not here acknowledged.

Further Reading

Andreyev Carlisle, Olga 'A Memoir of Childhood', *Island in Time* Holt Rhinehart (1980)

Bailey, Anthony *America Lost and Found*, Random House (1980)

Bles, Mark 'The True Story of a Belgian Resistance Fighter', *Child at War*, Mercury House (1991)

Dwark, D. 'Jewish youth in Nazi Europe', *Children With a Star* Yale University Press (1993)

Enser, A.G.S. *Subject Bibliography of the Second World War*, Oxford University Press

Estess, Ted L. *Elie Wiesel*, Frederick Ungar Publishing, New York (1994)

Gollomb and Taylor, *Young Heroes of the War*, The Vanguard Press, New York (1943)

Horne, Alistair *A Bundle From Britain*, St Martin's Press, New York (1994)

Houston, James D. and Wakatsuki Houston, Jeanne *Farewell to Manzanar*, Houghton Mifflin, New York and Boston (1973), Bantam Books (1974)

'A History of Everyday Life During the Second World War', *How We Lived Then* Hutchinson, London (1971)

Irons, Peter *Justice at War*, Oxford University Press, New York and Oxford (1983)

Jackson, Carlton *Who Will Take Our Children?*, Methuen, London (1985) British Evacuees

Kent, *Green Avalanche* (The story of an English girl's adventures as a combatant in World War II), Pythagorean (1960)

Kitagawa, Daisuke *Issei and Nisei: The Internment Years*, Seabury Press, New York (1967)

McAffee Brown, Robert *Elie Wiesel, Messenger to all Humanity*, University of Notre Dame (1983)

Miller, Russell *Resistance*, Time-Life Books, New York (1979)

The World At Arms (Illustrated history of World War II), Readers' Digest Books, New York (1989)

Tatieshi, John *And Justice For All: An Oral History of the Japanese American Detention Camps*, Random House, New York (1984)

Tuttle, William M. *Daddy's Gone to War* (The Second World War in the Lives of American Children), Jr. Oxford University Press (1993)

Wicks, Ben *No Time to Wave Goodbye*, St Martin's Press (1988) British Evacuees

Wiesel, Elie *From the Kingdom of Memory*, Simon and Schuster, New York (1990)

Wiesel, Elie *One Generation After*, Random House, New York (1965)